Eyewitness
AZTEC

Peruvian mummy cloth

Aztec sacrificial knife

Mesoamerican farming tools

Ceremonial urn showing Chac, the Mayan god of rain

Aztec ceramic flute

Marigolds, given as offerings to goddesses by the Aztecs

Moche vessel showing fisherman in boat

Peruvian silver portrait cup

Olmec jade mask

Eyewitness
AZTEC

Mortar and pestle
with chiles

Written by
ELIZABETH BAQUEDANO

Photographed by
MICHEL ZABÉ

Aztec army commander

Toltec coyote
warrior inlaid with
mother-of-pearl

Incan necklace made with
turquoise, shell, and gold beads

Aztec
skull mask

DK
DK Publishing

Warrior wearing feather headdress

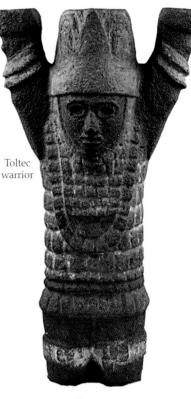

Toltec warrior

DK

LONDON, NEW YORK,
MELBOURNE, MUNICH, and DELHI

Project editor Christine Webb
Art editor Andrew Nash
Managing editor Helen Parker
Managing art editor Julia Harris
Production Louise Barratt
Picture research Cynthia Hole
Researcher Céline Carez
Additional photography Andy Crawford, Dave Rudkin

THIS EDITION
Editors Rob Houston, Steve Setford, Jessamy Wood
Art editors Carol Davis, Peter Radcliffe
Managing editors Julie Ferris, Jane Yorke
Managing art editor Owen Peyton Jones
Editorial director Nancy Ellwood
Associate publisher Andrew Macintyre
Production editor Marc Staples
US editor Margaret Parrish

This Eyewitness ® Guide has been conceived by
Dorling Kindersley Limited and Editions Gallimard

First published in the United States in 1993.
This revised edition published in the United States in 2011
by DK Publishing
375 Hudson Street, New York, New York 10014

A catalog record for this book is
available from the Library of Congress.

ISBN 978-0-7566-7320-8 (Hardcover)
ISBN 978-0-7566-8687-1 (Library Binding)

Color reproduction by Colourscan,
Singapore; MDP, UK

Printed and bound by Toppan Printing Co.
(Shenzhen) Ltd., China

Discover more at
www.dk.com

Peruvian
feather fan

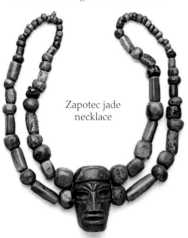

Zapotec jade
necklace

Mixtec head

Chancay
textile doll

Ancient Peruvian feather headdress

Contents

Chacmool from the Great Temple of the Aztecs

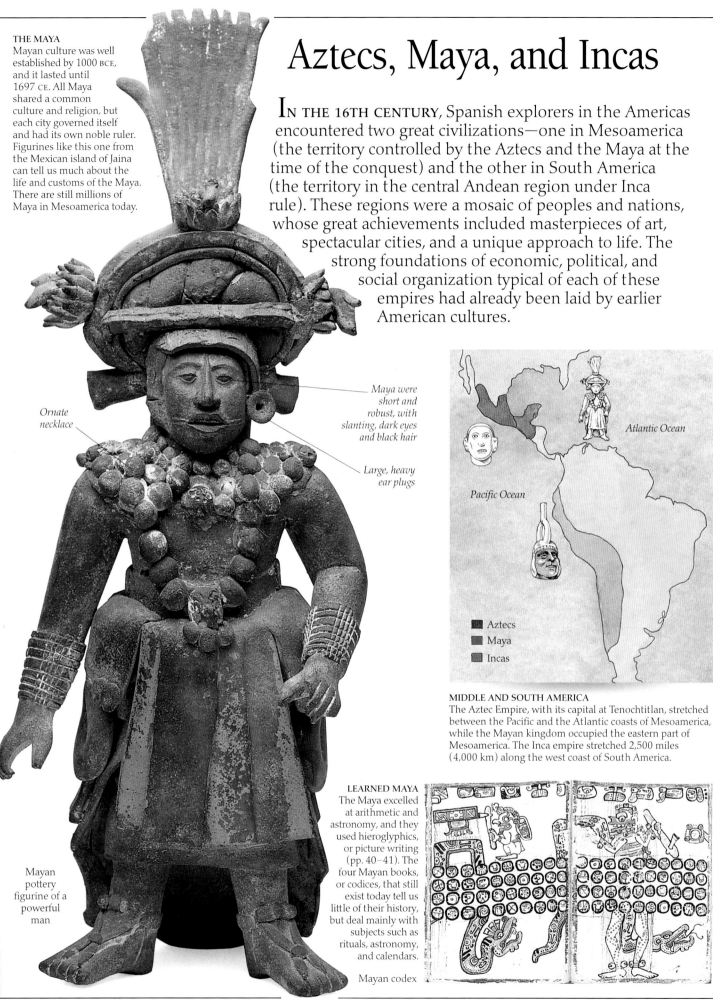

Aztecs, Maya, and Incas

IN THE 16TH CENTURY, Spanish explorers in the Americas encountered two great civilizations—one in Mesoamerica (the territory controlled by the Aztecs and the Maya at the time of the conquest) and the other in South America (the territory in the central Andean region under Inca rule). These regions were a mosaic of peoples and nations, whose great achievements included masterpieces of art, spectacular cities, and a unique approach to life. The strong foundations of economic, political, and social organization typical of each of these empires had already been laid by earlier American cultures.

THE MAYA
Mayan culture was well established by 1000 BCE, and it lasted until 1697 CE. All Maya shared a common culture and religion, but each city governed itself and had its own noble ruler. Figurines like this one from the Mexican island of Jaina can tell us much about the life and customs of the Maya. There are still millions of Maya in Mesoamerica today.

Ornate necklace

Maya were short and robust, with slanting, dark eyes and black hair

Large, heavy ear plugs

Atlantic Ocean

Pacific Ocean

- ■ Aztecs
- ■ Maya
- ■ Incas

MIDDLE AND SOUTH AMERICA
The Aztec Empire, with its capital at Tenochtitlan, stretched between the Pacific and the Atlantic coasts of Mesoamerica, while the Mayan kingdom occupied the eastern part of Mesoamerica. The Inca empire stretched 2,500 miles (4,000 km) along the west coast of South America.

Mayan pottery figurine of a powerful man

LEARNED MAYA
The Maya excelled at arithmetic and astronomy, and they used hieroglyphics, or picture writing (pp. 40–41). The four Mayan books, or codices, that still exist today tell us little of their history, but deal mainly with subjects such as rituals, astronomy, and calendars.

Mayan codex

THE FOUNDING OF TENOCHTITLAN

According to their mythology, Huitzilopochtli, the tribal god of the Aztecs, promised to show his people a place where they were to settle and build their great capital, Tenochtitlan. He told them to look for an eagle perched upon a cactus with a serpent in its beak. This first page of the Codex Mendoza (a book telling the history of the Aztecs) illustrates the foundation of Tenochtitlan in either 1325 or 1345. Mexico City is built on the same site.

INCA GOLD

The Incas excelled at working metals such as silver, copper, and gold (pp. 50–51). Female figures like this one have been found with Inca offerings to the gods.

Wooden cup, or *kero*, with decoration of an Inca man holding a spear and shield

THE AZTECS

The Aztecs were a wandering tribe before they settled in the Valley of Mexico on swampy land in Lake Texcoco and founded Tenochtitlan. The city grew in size and importance until it became the capital of the mighty Aztec Empire. The Aztecs conquered many peoples, demanding tribute from them (pp. 26–27). Aztecs were short and stocky, with brown skin and broad faces.

Aztecs had thick, black hair

THE ANDEAN PEOPLE

The Incan Empire became the most important state in the Andean highlands in 1438, when the Incas conquered the area around the city of Cuzco and made it their capital. They went on to occupy other provinces and incorporate them into their empire. Thanks to their efficient administration system, they were able to keep control of this vast domain. The people of the Andean area were typically small, with straight, black hair and brown skin.

Almond-shaped eyes

High cheekbones

Even white teeth

Aquiline nose

Stone sculpture of Aztec head

Moche pottery portrait vessel

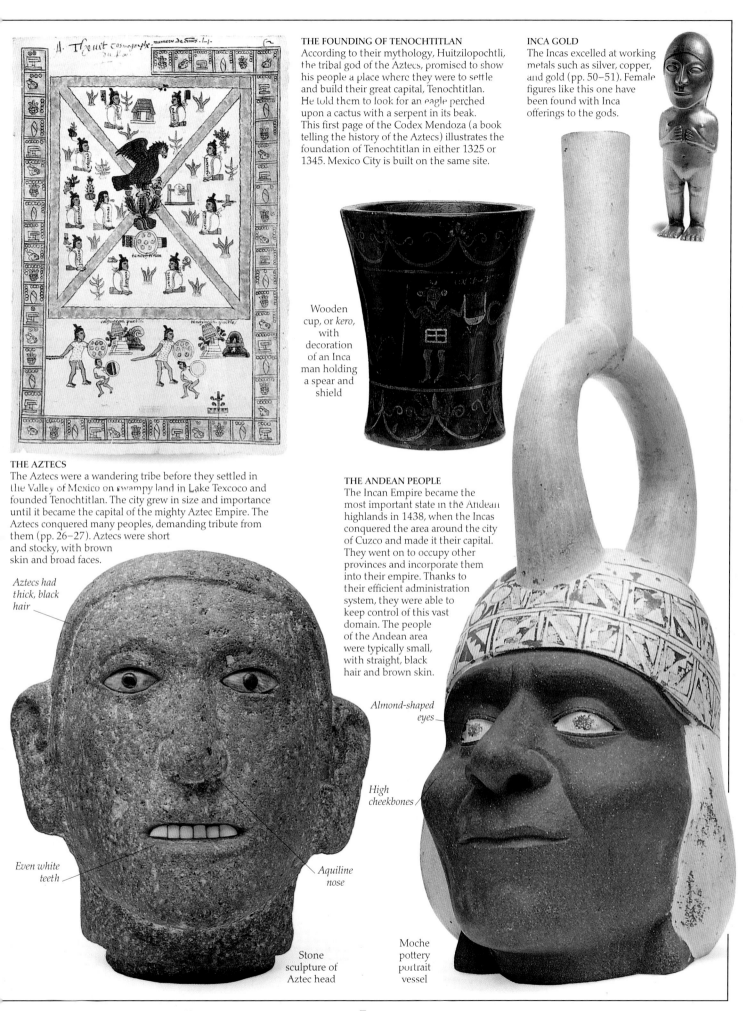

7

People of Mesoamerica

MESOAMERICA IS ONE OF two areas in the Americas (the other being the central Andes) that had urban civilizations at the time of the Spanish conquest in 1519. The fact that Mesoamerican people built spectacular pyramids and temples (pp. 30–31), had large markets (pp. 26–27), the ball game (pp. 58–59), a sacred calendar, hieroglyphic writing (pp. 40–41), several gods (pp. 32–33), and practiced human sacrifice (pp. 36–37) sets Mesoamerica apart from its neighbors. Mesoamerican cultural history is divided into three main periods: the Preclassic or Formative, the Classic, and the Postclassic, which together stretched from about 2000 BCE until the Spanish conquest (pp. 62–63). During these periods, Mesoamerica saw the rise and fall of many civilizations. In the Preclassic Period, the Olmecs were the dominant culture. The Classic Period witnessed the rise of the Teotihuacan culture and the Maya. The Postclassic Period was a time of strife and warring empires, such as those of the Toltecs and Aztecs.

WARRING AZTECS
At its height, the Aztec Empire was strong and prosperous. Conquered areas were controlled by the powerful Aztec army. This illustration shows an army commander.

MAYAN RITUAL
Religion was the center of every Mayan person's life. One of the major achievements of the Maya was the construction of superb temples and other buildings to honor their gods. These were decorated with carvings, as can be seen on this lintel showing a woman drawing blood from her tongue. Self-sacrifice was common throughout Mesoamerica.

MAP OF MESOAMERICA
Mesoamerica is both a geographical and a cultural region. At the time of the Spanish conquest, it included what is now central and southern Mexico and the peninsula of Yucatán, Guatemala, Belize, El Salvador, the westernmost part of Honduras, and a small part of Nicaragua and northern Costa Rica.

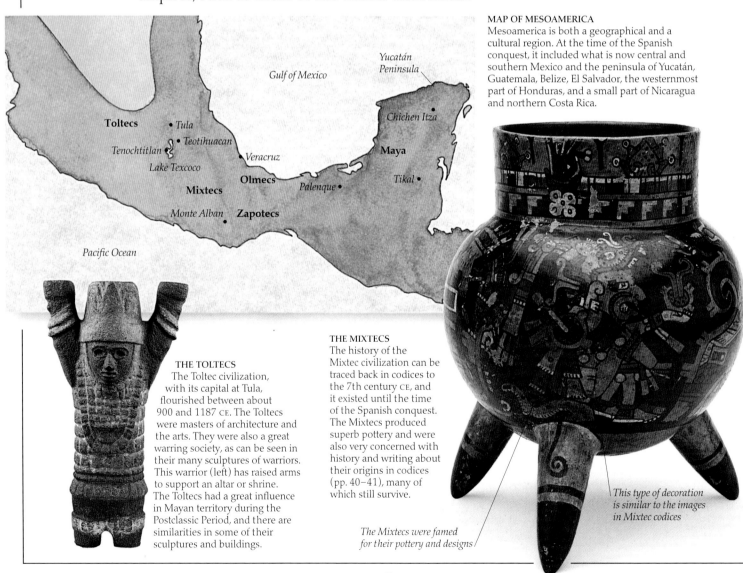

Gulf of Mexico

Yucatán Peninsula

Toltecs • Tula • Teotihuacan

Tenochtitlan

Lake Texcoco

Veracruz

Chichen Itza

Maya

Mixtecs

Olmecs

Palenque

Tikal •

Monte Alban Zapotecs

Pacific Ocean

THE TOLTECS
The Toltec civilization, with its capital at Tula, flourished between about 900 and 1187 CE. The Toltecs were masters of architecture and the arts. They were also a great warring society, as can be seen in their many sculptures of warriors. This warrior (left) has raised arms to support an altar or shrine. The Toltecs had a great influence in Mayan territory during the Postclassic Period, and there are similarities in some of their sculptures and buildings.

THE MIXTECS
The history of the Mixtec civilization can be traced back in codices to the 7th century CE, and it existed until the time of the Spanish conquest. The Mixtecs produced superb pottery and were also very concerned with history and writing about their origins in codices (pp. 40–41), many of which still survive.

The Mixtecs were famed for their pottery and designs

This type of decoration is similar to the images in Mixtec codices

TEOTIHUACAN
The Teotihuacan culture—the most influential in Mesoamerica—flourished between 1 and 750 CE. The city of Teotihuacan is the most impressive ancient city in the Americas. We know little about the physical appearance of its people, but masks found at Teotihuacan give us some idea of what they looked like.

Head made of basalt is 5 ft (1.5 m) tall and weighs more than 20 tons

COLOSSAL HEAD
Several heads like this one have been found in the Olmec heartland in Mexico's Gulf Coast region. They may represent rulers or important people.

Hole in earlobe for earring

Masks may have been portraits of the dead

Greenstone mask from Teotihuacan

THE OLMECS
The Olmec civilization flourished between about 1200 and 200 BCE. Their legacy to other cultures in Mesoamerica included platform mounds, plazas, ball courts, and hieroglyphic (picture) writing. Olmec artifacts have been found in many parts of Mesoamerica. Their art is naturalistic and symbolic. This figurine seems to represent a bald-headed baby.

Facial features similar to peoples of Southeast Asia

Zapotec nobleman trying on jeweled headdress, detail from a painting by Diego Rivera called *Cultivation of Maize*

ZAPOTEC CIVILIZATION
The Zapotecs, with their capital at Monte Alban, were established in about 600 BCE and declined around 800 CE. The Zapotec state was one of the largest at the time in Mesoamerica. The Zapotecs excelled in the art of featherwork and manufacturing gold jewelry.

Olmec figurine of a bald-headed baby

The Incas and their ancestors

BEFORE THE INCA EMPIRE reached its peak in South America, many Andean cultures had already laid the framework for its success. These cultures left no written records of their history, and all that is known of them comes from the study of their architecture, pottery, and the remains found in their graves. Archeologists have identified separate periods of cultural growth culminating with the Incas. The first complex societies were formed in around 1800 BCE. Between this time and the rise of the Incas in the mid 15th century CE, various cultures emerged, gradually becoming highly organized civilizations with social structures, political and economic systems, specialized artisans, and a religion in which many gods were worshiped. Along the desert coast of Peru there were civilized states such as the Nazca, the Moche, and the Chimu. In the highlands, the Huari and the Tiahuanaco were complex and organized cultures. Between 1438 and 1534 CE, all of these elements were brought together and improved on under the Incan Empire.

NAZCA
The Nazca inhabited the southern coastal valleys of Peru from 300 BCE to 600 CE. They were well-known for their arts, which included textiles and metalwork. But the real hallmark of the Nazca civilization is its painted pottery, decorated with realistic and mythological scenes.

INCA NOBLES
The scenes painted on vessels and other objects help us learn more about Andean life and culture. For example, Inca nobles usually carried a lance, as this painting on a wooden cup, or *kero*, shows.

MOCHE
The Moche people flourished on the northern desert coast of Peru between about 100 CE and 700 CE. They were skilled weavers and goldsmiths, and remarkable potters. Their representations of people, plants, animals, and gods in a wide range of activities give us an insight into their lives.

Moche person of high status wearing headband with jaguar decoration and earplugs

TIAHUANACO
The Tiahuanaco Empire of the Peruvian–Bolivian Altiplano (southern Peru and northwestern Bolivia) flourished between about 500 and 750 CE. It was a strong state with an impressive ceremonial center.

Tiahuanaco pottery jaguar

HUARI
The Huari (500 to 900 CE) were neighbors of the Tiahuanaco. Their state was highly organized, with an advanced irrigation system and a distinctive architectural style. It expanded by conquering neighboring areas. Many Huari ideas, including pottery techniques, were adopted by other Andean cultures. The Huari also had their own style of art. A common theme is an "angel" figure with wings, as seen here.

The Tiahuanaco and the Huari art styles shared many of the same symbols, especially of the cat family

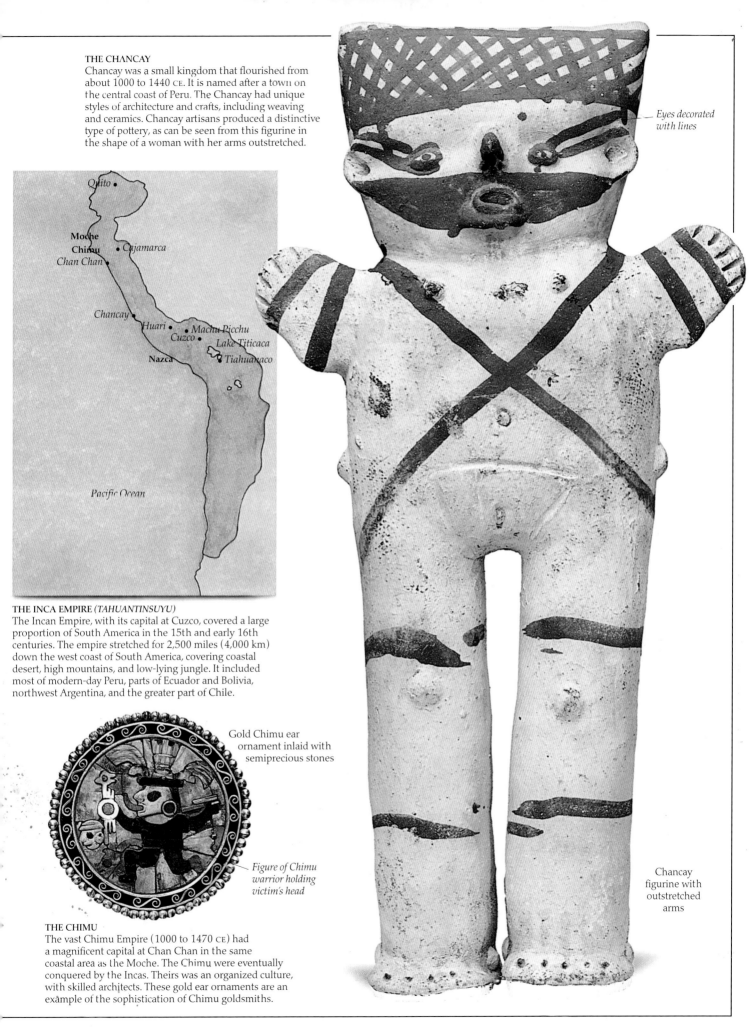

THE CHANCAY
Chancay was a small kingdom that flourished from about 1000 to 1440 CE. It is named after a town on the central coast of Peru. The Chancay had unique styles of architecture and crafts, including weaving and ceramics. Chancay artisans produced a distinctive type of pottery, as can be seen from this figurine in the shape of a woman with her arms outstretched.

Quito

Moche
Chimu · Cajamarca
Chan Chan

Chancay ·
Huari · · Machu Picchu
Cuzco ·
Lake Titicaca
Nazca · Tiahuanaco

Pacific Ocean

THE INCA EMPIRE (TAHUANTINSUYU)
The Incan Empire, with its capital at Cuzco, covered a large proportion of South America in the 15th and early 16th centuries. The empire stretched for 2,500 miles (4,000 km) down the west coast of South America, covering coastal desert, high mountains, and low-lying jungle. It included most of modern-day Peru, parts of Ecuador and Bolivia, northwest Argentina, and the greater part of Chile.

Gold Chimu ear ornament inlaid with semiprecious stones

Figure of Chimu warrior holding victim's head

THE CHIMU
The vast Chimu Empire (1000 to 1470 CE) had a magnificent capital at Chan Chan in the same coastal area as the Moche. The Chimu were eventually conquered by the Incas. Theirs was an organized culture, with skilled architects. These gold ear ornaments are an example of the sophistication of Chimu goldsmiths.

Eyes decorated with lines

Chancay figurine with outstretched arms

Farming

AGRICULTURE WAS A VITAL PART of life for the ancient Americans. Their farmers used sophisticated methods of cultivation, and by the time of the Spanish conquest (p. 62) they were the greatest plant cultivators in the world. Corn from Mesoamerica and potatoes from the Andes (pp. 24–25) were some of their contributions to the European diet. Human labor was the vital ingredient in both regions. There were no animals for carrying loads or plows in Mesoamerica, and although the Andean people had the llama, it could only carry very small loads. Farming methods varied according to the climate and geography of the area. The Aztecs grew their most productive crops on the *chinampas*— plots of fertile land built in swampy lakes.

GODDESS OF AGRICULTURE
This incense burner (used to burn a resin called *copal*) represents an agricultural goddess. Agricultural goddesses were often adorned with a pleated fan, like this one.

BUILDING *CHINAMPAS*
Chinampas were made by staking out narrow, rectangular strips in marshy lakes. Narrow canals were built between them for canoes to pass along. Each *chinampa* was built up with layers of thick water vegetation cut from the lake's surface and mud from the bottom of the lake. They were piled up like mats to make the plots. Willow trees were planted around the edge of each *chinampa* to make it more secure.

FERTILE PLOTS
Crops of vegetables and flowers were grown on the fertile *chinampas*, along with medicinal plants and herbs.

Rich soil from the bottom of the lake was used as fertilizer

Corn

Long, broad blade

FARMER'S TOOL
The digging stick, or _uictli_, was the essential farmer's tool. Digging sticks were used for various jobs, such as hoeing and planting.

DIGGING STICK
Digging sticks were made with the strongest and longest-lasting woods.

HARVESTTIME
Life in Mesoamerica and the Andean region revolved around the cycles of planting, cultivating, and harvesting crops such as corn.

PLANTING THE SEED
This illustration from the Florentine Codex shows an Aztec farmer planting corn using a digging stick.

Stone head

Wooden handle

CORN CROP
Corn was the staple food of the Maya as well as the Aztecs. It is still an important crop today.

AX
Axes were used for chopping or hammering.

Nazca pot showing a farmer holding plants

CORNCOB VESSEL
Andean pottery was often made in the shape of the fruits and vegetables that were grown. Corn originated in Mesoamerica, but was widely grown in the Americas.

Head attached to handle with cord

HOE
This tool was used as a spade to turn the soil of the plots.

TERRACES AT MACHU PICCHU
To get the highest yield from their crops, the Incas used sophisticated terracing and irrigation methods on hillsides in the highlands. Building terraces meant that they could use more land for cultivation, and also helped to resist erosion of the land by wind and rain.

TENDING CROPS
In the Andean region, cultivating the soil was the basis of life. Farmers tended their crops using simple tools such as a digging stick, a clod breaker, and a hoe.

JADE FISH
People from coastal regions drew inspiration from fish and marine life to decorate pottery and jade objects.

Hunting and fishing

HUNTING AND FISHING were important activities in Mesoamerica and in the Andean regions. Meat and fish were part of the diet, especially in the Andean region, depending on what was available in the area. Animal life in the Andes was most abundant in the high mountains of the north, where large mammals such as deer and vicuñas (wild relatives of the llama) roamed. In Mesoamerica, the largest animals were the peccary (a relative of the pig) and the deer, which were hunted with bows and arrows. Dogs, rabbits, and other small animals were also eaten. Mesoamericans and South Americans fished for everything from shellfish to large fish and sea mammals using nets, harpoons, and angling. They made fishing hooks from sturdy cactus thorns, shell, and bone. Hooks were also made of copper in South America.

IN THE NET
Catching waterfowl in nets was widespread in Mesoamerica's lake areas.

FISHING NET
The lake system in and around Tenochtitlan provided people with fish and waterfowl, fresh water for drinking, and irrigation for crops. Sometimes fish were transported in canoes to markets and sold. Many nets in present-day Mexico are similar to those produced by the Aztecs and other Mesoamerican peoples. The most common net used by the Aztecs was bag-shaped, like this one, and made of fibers from the agave plant.

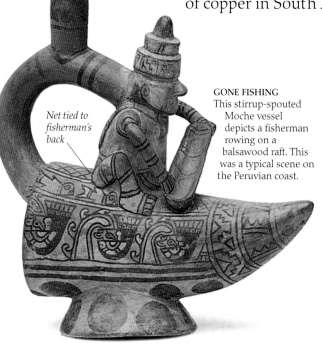

Net tied to fisherman's back

GONE FISHING
This stirrup-spouted Moche vessel depicts a fisherman rowing on a balsawood raft. This was a typical scene on the Peruvian coast.

FAMILY TRADITION
Many trades, such as fishing, were passed from father to son. Boys were taught to fish when very young, and at the age of 14 they went out fishing alone.

Raft is made from woven reeds—the Aztecs and Maya made their canoes from hollowed-out tree trunks

REED RAFT
Watercraft were fashioned from reeds because of the shortage of wood in areas where few or no trees grew. This type of raft was—and still is— used high in the Andes around Lake Titicaca and also on the coast. Large rafts between 14 ft 6 in and 20 ft (4.5 m and 6.1 m) long were equipped with a wooden mast for raising and lowering the sail made of reeds.

DEER-HUNTING SCENE
This beautiful Mayan plate from Yucatán, decorated with black and bright orange paints, shows a lively hunting scene. The hunter at the center has already captured a deer, which he carries draped over his head and back. Surrounding this central image are other hunters wearing deer masks in an attempt to distract the animal they want to catch.

Hunter carrying deer

Hunter disguised as prey

FATAL WEAPON
Slings were used as long-range weapons by both Inca hunters and soldiers. They were made from braided llama wool. The stone was placed in a small cradle. Holding both ends, the sling was whirled around the head. Releasing one end sent the stone hurtling toward its target with great accuracy. The injury inflicted by the stone could be fatal.

Stone placed in braided woolen cradle

A BIRD IN THE HAND
The art of the ancient South American people shows us what their activities were. This wooden cup is painted with a scene of a man hunting birds.

BOW AND ARROW *right*
Bows, arrows, and spear throwers (below) were weapons used originally in Central Mexico, and later introduced to the Mayan area. Along with the javelin and the sling, the bow and arrow were used for hunting animals at long range.

Bow

SHOOTING FISH
The Maya caught fish in lagoons using bows and arrows.

Arrow

Arrow head made from obsidian

Spear

NAZCA FOX
This fox was part of the decoration on a Nazca pot. Foxes usually symbolized war. They were also considered pests and were killed mainly with clubs.

SPEAR AND SPEAR THROWER
Spears (above) had a fire-hardened tip or a point made of chipped stone or obsidian. They were propelled by a spear thrower, or *atlatl* (below). This was a long piece of wood with a groove down the center.

Spear thrower

Finger holes for gripping spear thrower

The shaft of the spear rested in this groove

Mesoamerican cities

THE PEOPLES OF MESOAMERICA established their cities in a variety of geographic and climatic areas. Some were located in the highlands, others in jungles or coastal regions. The Olmecs built their cities in tropical regions, while the people of Teotihuacan, the Toltecs, and the Aztecs founded theirs in the highlands. Mayan cities were set up in both highland and lowland regions. These geographical differences influenced the architecture of the cities. As time passed, the cities grew in size. The Olmecs (1200 BC) lived in small cities, but Teotihuacan (200 CE) had an estimated 150,000 inhabitants or more. The central areas of Mesoamerican cities were reserved for religious and public buildings, and for the houses of rulers and of the elite. The homes of ordinary people were built outside these areas.

CHICHEN ITZA

The Mayan city of Chichen Itza was built at a strategic location in the center of the Yucatán Peninsula. Chichen Itza grew into an important commercial center that maintained links with many other areas. It is thought that the Toltecs of highland Central Mexico later established themselves at Chichen Itza.

Temple-pyramid *El Castillo* (The Castle) at Chichen Itza

TRIBUTE TOWNS

The Codex Mendoza (p. 7) gives the names of towns that paid tribute to Tenochtitlan, as well as the goods required. Each of these glyphs (left) represents the name of a subject town.

PALENQUE

This Mayan temple is situated in Palenque, in the midst of tropical jungle. Hidden in the pyramid was the funeral chamber of Lord Pacal (p. 53), who ruled for 68 years and was buried in this magnificent resting place in 683 CE. His sarcophagus (stone coffin) contained some of the most beautiful jade objects ever found in Mesoamerica.

Temple of the Inscriptions at Palenque

Shrine to Tlaloc, god of rain

Great Temple of the Aztecs

Temple steps

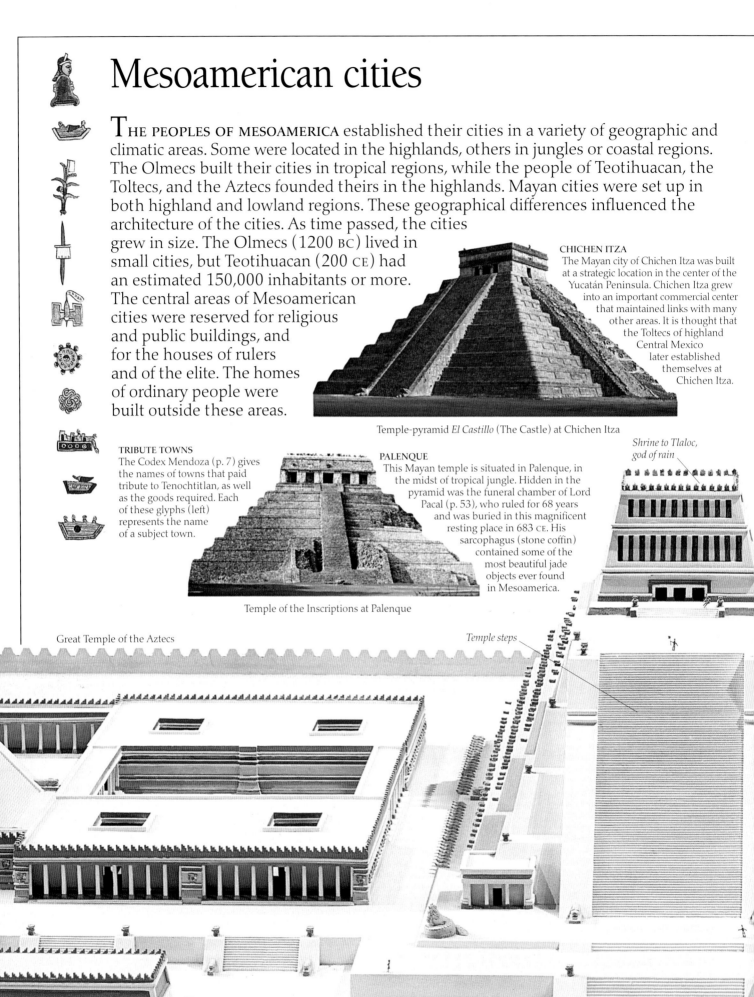

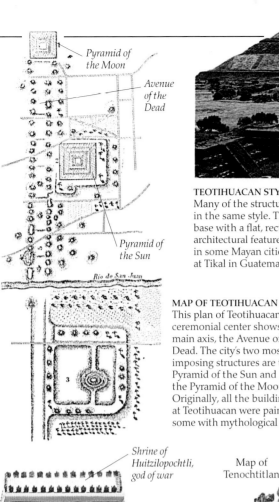

Pyramid of
the Moon

*Avenue
of the
Dead*

Pyramid of
the Sun

Rio de San Juan

TEOTIHUACAN STYLE
Many of the structures at Teotihuacan were built
in the same style. They consisted of a sloping
base with a flat, rectangular top. This
architectural feature is also found
in some Mayan cities, such as
at Tikal in Guatemala.

MAP OF TEOTIHUACAN
This plan of Teotihuacan's
ceremonial center shows its
main axis, the Avenue of the
Dead. The city's two most
imposing structures are the
Pyramid of the Sun and
the Pyramid of the Moon.
Originally, all the buildings
at Teotihuacan were painted,
some with mythological scenes.

TOLTEC WARRIOR
This is one of the warriors
on the top of Temple B at
Tula. These warriors once
supported a roof. The
warrior is equipped with
a spear thrower, and his
breastplate in the shape
of a butterfly indicates
that he is a warrior.

Temple B, or the Temple
of Quetzalcoatl, at Tula

TULA
The Toltec capital of Tula reflects the beginning
of an era of great military action. Despite Tula
being the capital of the god Quetzalcoatl, who
was opposed to war and human sacrifice, there
are carvings of warriors equipped for war
everywhere, including on top of temple pyramids.

*Shrine of
Huitzilopochtli,
god of war*

Map of
Tenochtitlan

*Skulls of
sacrificed victims*

Brazier

TENOCHTITLAN
This European map (left) shows Tenochtitlan, the
physical and spiritual heart of the Aztec Empire.
The city was built on a lake and was reached by
causeways, or raised roads. The Spanish conquerors,
or *conquistadores*, described the streets as being large,
wide, and straight. The Great Temple of the Aztecs
(pp. 30–31) was at the city's center. The model
below shows the Great Temple inside the sacred
precinct. It had shrines to both Tlaloc, god of rain,
and Huitzilopochtli, god of war, who was also the
god of the Aztecs. Just outside the ceremonial
center there were palaces, warrior schools,
shrines, and a ball court (pp. 58–59).

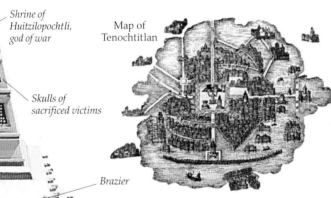

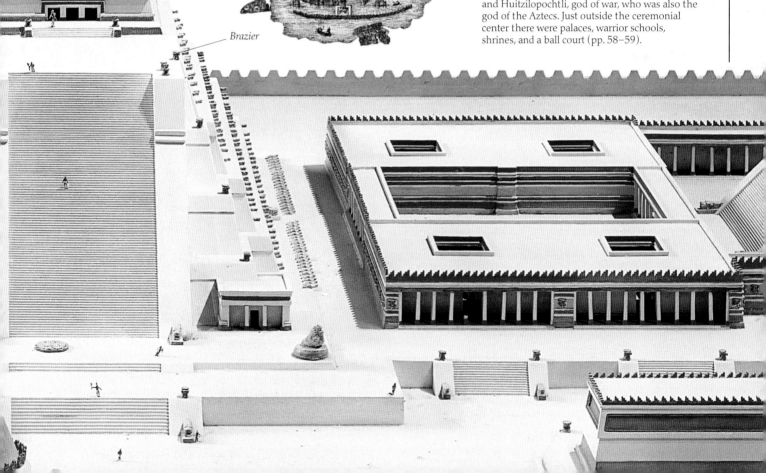

Cities of the Andes

Gateway of the Sun at Tiahuanaco

THE PEOPLE OF THE ANDEAN REGION lived either in highland or coastal areas. They built their cities to suit the location, using materials that were locally available. Typical highland buildings had sloping, thatched roofs and masonry walls. Buildings on the coast tended to have flat roofs and mud-brick (adobe) walls covered by painted mud plaster. Highland cities, such as Machu Picchu, could not be built on a regular grid plan like Chan Chan and other cities in flat, coastal areas. The first buildings to be lived in as homes date back to the 4th century BCE. Government buildings, storehouses, bridges, canals, and other public constructions were built by ordinary people as a kind of labor tax, with the state providing the necessary materials.

INCA MASONS
The Incas are renowned for their fine stonework. Masons cut huge, stone bricks using just a stone hammer and then polished them with wet sand. The bricks fit together so closely that no mortar was needed.

TIAHUANACO
The city of Tiahuanaco (p. 10) is situated on a high plain nearly 13,000 ft (4,000 m) above sea level and rimmed by the Andes Mountains. The stunning architecture of its ceremonial center included an impressive number of stone sculptures. The Gateway of the Sun (above) was carved from a single block of stone. A carving over the doorway portrays a Sun god.

OLLANTAYTAMBO
The Inca town of Ollantaytambo has some of Peru's most impressive architectural remains. This doorway is made of rectangular stone blocks, each precisely cut and fit to a specific position.

Royal compound at Chan Chan, capital of the Chimu kingdom

Bird motif on adobe wall of royal compound, Chan Chan

ADOBE DECORATION
The Chimu decorated their thick adobe (mud) walls with molded motifs, usually associated with the sea , such as birds, fish, and men in boats.

CHAN CHAN
The Chimu people built real urban centers, and Chan Chan, the coastal capital of the Chimu Empire, is a good example of this. The city was organized on a grid plan and covered approximately 2.3 sq miles (6 sq km). It contained 10 compounds, each enclosed by a high adobe wall. These are thought to be the royal residences and administrative centers of the Chimu kings. Each king lived, died, and was buried in his own secluded compound.

European map of Cuzco

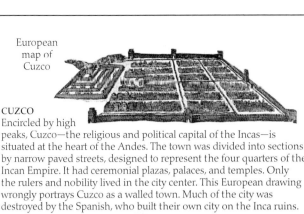

CUZCO

Encircled by high peaks, Cuzco—the religious and political capital of the Incas—is situated at the heart of the Andes. The town was divided into sections by narrow paved streets, designed to represent the four quarters of the Incan Empire. It had ceremonial plazas, palaces, and temples. Only the rulers and nobility lived in the city center. This European drawing wrongly portrays Cuzco as a walled town. Much of the city was destroyed by the Spanish, who built their own city on the Inca ruins.

Stone walls of Sacsahuaman fort

SACSAHUAMAN FORT

Cuzco was protected from the enemy by the fortress of Sacsahuaman, built on a steep hill overlooking the city from the north. The fort was constructed with locally quarried stone, and each giant block was individually shaped. These three impressive stone walls, which stand 52 ft (16 m) high, guarded the fortress.

Inca baths at Tambomachay

INCA BATHS

Inca palaces sometimes had sunken stone baths in which the kings could relax and bathe. Water ran along stone channels into the baths. These baths at Tambomachay, near Cuzco, were built at the site of a sacred spring. They were used by the Inca kings.

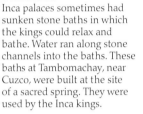

Machu Picchu

MACHU PICCHU

Strategically positioned at the edge of the Incan Empire, the remote city of Machu Picchu was probably built in the mid to late 15th century. The Spanish *conquistadores* never found Machu Picchu, and the city was not discovered until 1911. The site is an outstanding example of Incan architecture—a natural fortress protected by steep slopes, surrounded by high mountain peaks and approached from only one direction. Of its 143 granite buildings, about 80 were houses and the rest were ceremonial buildings such as temples. Many mummies were found at Machu Picchu, most of them women.

Family life

THE MESOAMERICAN MAN, as a husband and father, was responsible for the well-being of his household. He was expected to support his family, as well as his government, through hard work and by paying taxes. The woman, as a wife and mother, devoted her time and energy to running her household and caring for her children. Girls were taught domestic chores, such as weaving and cooking, and sons followed their fathers while they worked. Children had free schooling, and nobles had their own schools. Family life was similar in the Andean region. The father worked to support the family and pay taxes; the mother worked in the home, helped her husband with his work, and cared for the children. Incan commoners had to educate their own children.

COUPLE EMBRACING
In both Mesoamerica and the Andean region, a wife's role was to obey her husband. Even in art, women were often depicted in a passive stance, and men in a more active position. This Mayan pottery statue shows a man embracing a woman. Both wear elaborate headdresses, ear plugs, and necklaces indicating that the they were a wealthy couple.

Figure has eyes and teeth inlaid with shell

Aztec couple during marriage ceremony

JUST MARRIED
One of the rituals in an Aztec wedding ceremony was to tie the young man's cloak and the girl's blouse together. The wedding party took place afterward, with dancing and singing.

FERTILE BLESSING
Both the Mesoamericans and the Incas considered it important for a married couple to have children. The Aztecs worshiped goddesses of fertility. This wooden Aztec sculpture is of a young woman dressed in a skirt and bare-breasted. She may be a goddess of fertility.

CELEBRATION
There were great celebrations when an Aztec baby was born. The festivities lasted for days, during which astrologers checked to see when would be a favorable day for the baby to be named.

Stirrup handle

Two helpers aid a woman giving birth

CHILDBIRTH SCENE
The Aztecs did not have midwives. When giving birth, Andean women were helped by women who had given birth to twins, and also by their neighbors. After the birth, the mother washed herself and her baby in the river. The umbilical cord was not thrown away, but was kept in the house.

BRINGING UP BABIES
Family scenes are common in Aztec art and show women performing various activities. This woman is carrying two children, one under each arm. One of the main roles of an Aztec woman was to bring up her children until they were ready to leave home and marry.

Steam made by throwing water on walls of bath house

WOMAN CARRYING LOAD
The duties of women in the Andean region varied according to their rank. The woman depicted in this Moche vessel was probably a commoner's wife and was expected to help her husband when necessary. This included carrying heavy loads on her back. She wears a strap called a trump line that passes around her forehead to hold the load on her back.

Trump line, or strap, helped people to carry heavy loads

Fire for heating steam bath

STEAM BATHS
Bathing was a part of the daily family routine of the Aztecs, both for keeping clean and for purification. Almost every home had a steam bath alongside it. The bath house was a small building that was heated by a fireplace. When water was thrown on the hot inside walls, the room filled with steam.

PUNISHMENT
From the age of 11 years, disobedient Aztec children were punished in various ways by their parents. Punishments included pricking their skin with spines and making them inhale the smoke from burning chile peppers.

CHILD'S PLAY
Until they were old enough to help their parents with their work, children played in and around the home. This pottery toy is in the form of a dog on wheels. Toys like this show that the peoples of Mesoamerica knew about the wheel. However, they used it for decorative purposes rather than practical ones, and they had no wheeled wagons to help them carry loads. Wheeled toys have been found mainly in graves in parts of the Gulf of Mexico. Toys in the form of dogs may have been thought to help the soul of the dead person to find his or her resting place in the afterlife.

Collar

Wheel turns on bolt

At home

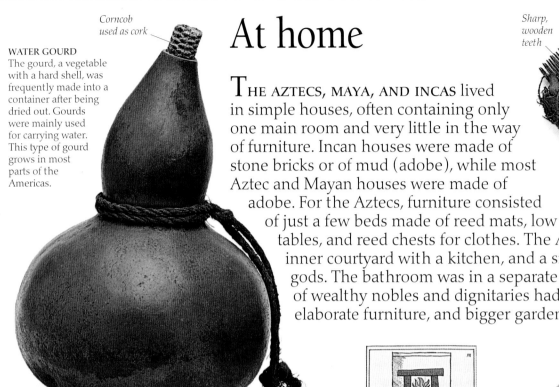

WATER GOURD
The gourd, a vegetable with a hard shell, was frequently made into a container after being dried out. Gourds were mainly used for carrying water. This type of gourd grows in most parts of the Americas.

Corncob used as cork

Sharp, wooden teeth

HANDY TOOL
Combs were made of bone or wood. They were used for hairdressing and, in South America, for preparing wool. Some were even used to make patterns on pottery.

THE AZTECS, MAYA, AND INCAS lived in simple houses, often containing only one main room and very little in the way of furniture. Incan houses were made of stone bricks or of mud (adobe), while most Aztec and Mayan houses were made of adobe. For the Aztecs, furniture consisted of just a few beds made of reed mats, low tables, and reed chests for clothes. The Aztec home had an inner courtyard with a kitchen, and a small shrine to the gods. The bathroom was in a separate building. The homes of wealthy nobles and dignitaries had more rooms, more elaborate furniture, and bigger gardens.

REED MAT
Mesoamerican people sat, played, and slept on reed mats. This type of mat would have been used as a rug on the floor of most houses. Other, thicker mats were used as beds. Both rich and poor homes had mats like the one above.

INSIDE AN AZTEC HOUSE
An Aztec woman's home meant almost everything to her. She spent most of her day in the house, looking after the children, cooking, or weaving.

MULTIPURPOSE POT
This pot was used to store liquids and food. It was stood on a ring made of reeds to keep it upright.

Bowl has three sturdy legs

TRIPOD BOWL
Potters working in Teotihuacan often made three-legged bowls like this, sometimes with a lid. Pots for day-to-day use were usually plain, but others had a pattern, either cut into the surface or painted on, as here.

INCAN HOUSE
Incan doors and windows were shaped like a trapezium—four-sided, but with only two parallel sides

The most common type of Incan house, whether made from adobe or stone, was rectangular with a thatched roof, and usually had just one room. There was no furniture in an Incan house. The stone blocks used to build houses were carved so that that they fit together perfectly, and there was no need for cement.

CURVED KNIFE
Knives with metal blades of various shapes were known as *tumi*. This Peruvian *tumi* is made of copper with a fitted bone handle.

Curved blade may have been used for cutting up food

End of handle is in the shape of an animal's head

Chisel has a wooden handle carved in the shape of a jaguar

HOW PEOPLE LIVED
This pot was found in an ancient Peruvian grave. It is an elaborate, decorated version of the type of pot that would have been used in the Andean region for everyday cooking and eating. Objects found in graves give us an idea of how people lived long ago.

JAGUAR CHISEL
Everyday Andean tools, such as this chisel, have been found in sacred places, or *huacas*.

GRINDING STONE
Early every morning, the women would revive the hearth fire and grind corn on the grinding stone, or *metlatl* (made of volcanic stone, usually basalt). Grinding stones were basic tools in the kitchen. Today, grinding stones are still used throughout the Mesoamerican region, mainly for grinding corn into flour.

Cylindrical stone used to press the corn against the grinding stone

Vessels with stirrup spouts such as this one were made only in South America

Water pot in the shape of a Moche building

HIGH-CLASS VESSEL
In the Andean region, a person's status could be told by the kind of drinking vessel he or she used. Peasants drank from gourd bowls, while the well-to-do drank from pottery containers like the one shown here. Some wealthy people drank from gold or silver vessels.

Food and drink

THE MESOAMERICANS AND ANDEANS ate simply. Corn was the central food in their diet, along with vegetables such as beans and squashes. Not all foods were grown in both regions, however. Potatoes and quinoa (a grain) came from the Andean region, while avocados and tomatoes were mainly consumed in Mesoamerica, along with a wide variety of fruit. Corn was made into a sort of porridge, called *atole* in Mesoamerica and *capia* in Incan territory. Corn cakes were eaten in both regions, but only the Mesoamerican peoples ate corn pancakes known as *tortillas* with every meal. A favorite dish among the Aztecs and Incas was *tamales*, a kind of envelope of steamed corn stuffed with vegetables or meat. In both Mesoamerica and the Andean region, it was customary for people to eat twice a day; the Mesoamericans ate their main meal during the hottest part of the day.

Guinea pig meat was the only meat regularly eaten by the Andeans.

Cocoa beans

Chocolate was made with ground cocoa beans and water

COCOA
A chocolate drink made from cocoa was drunk by wealthy Mesoamericans. It was sweetened with honey and flavored with vanilla.

Cocoa pod

Bowl-shaped stone mortar

Pestle, shaped like a club

MORTAR AND PESTLE
Chiles and tomatoes were used for making sauces. They were crushed with a stone called a pestle in a mortar, which was a stone bowl that stood on three small feet.

Comal

TORTILLAS
The Mesoamerican diet is still centered around *tortillas*. Once the *tortillas* have been made, they are cooked over the fire on a pottery disk called a *comal*.

WOMEN PREPARING CORN
The preparation of corn was a daily task for Mesoamerican women. This section of a painting by the Mexican artist Diego Rivera shows a woman grinding corn kernels into flour between a stone roller and slab. The flour is made into a dough, which another woman pats into *tortillas*.

LLAMA
The tender meat of the llama was eaten by the Incas and their ancestors. However, they ate it in moderation, since the llama was useful as a pack animal and it also provided wool for textiles.

Llama tied up with ropes

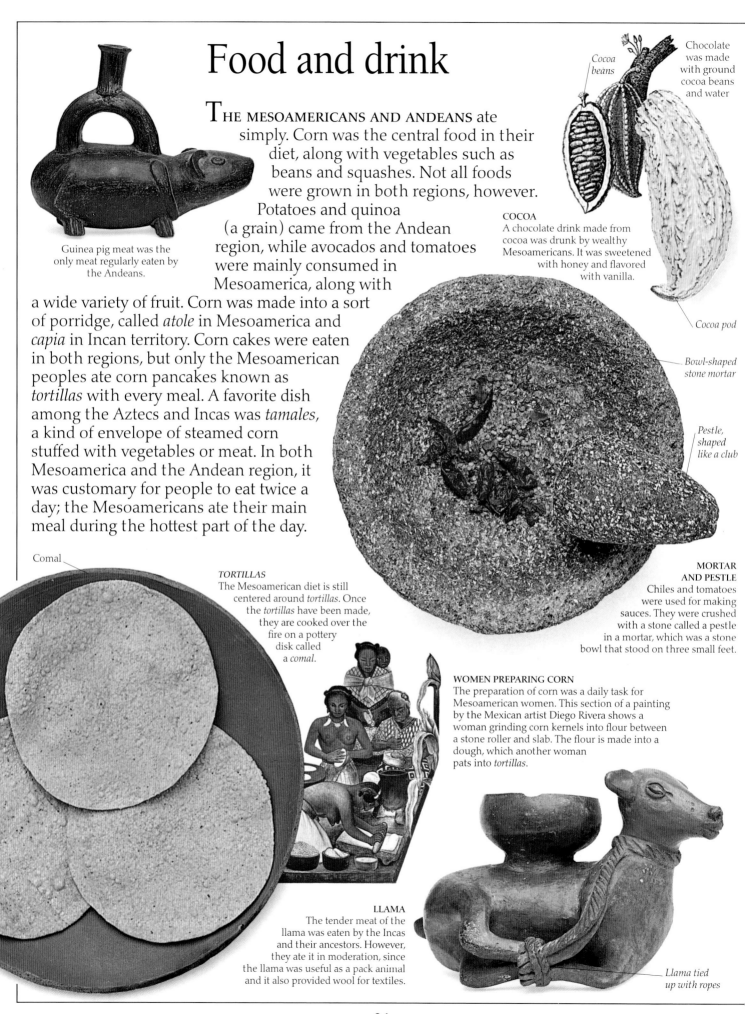

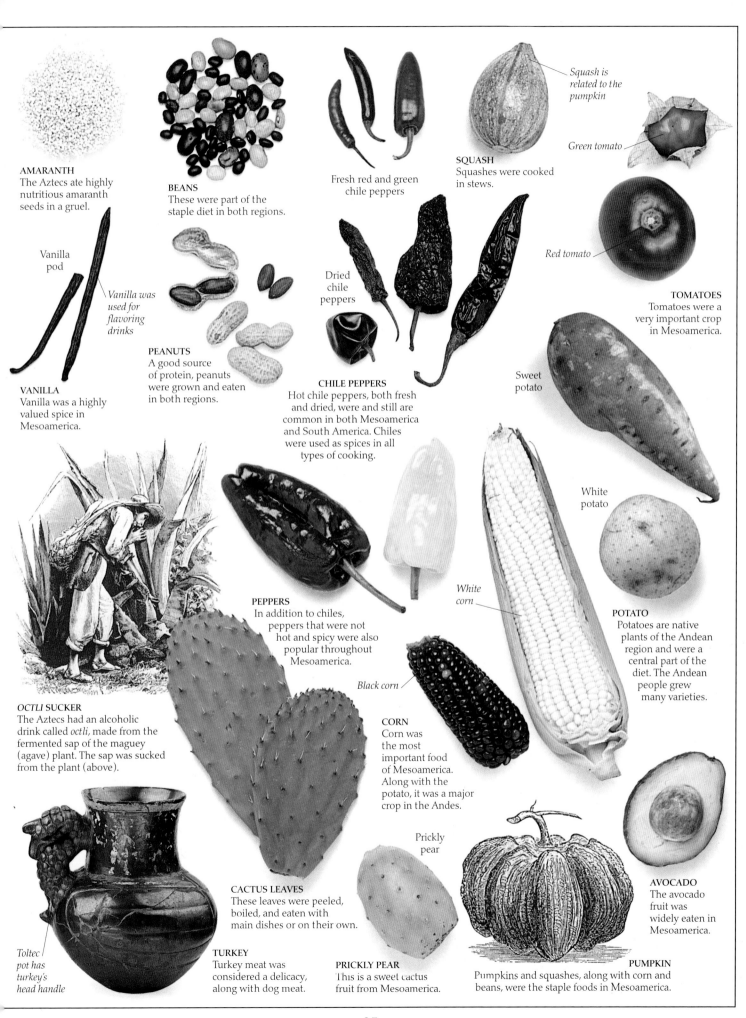

AMARANTH
The Aztecs ate highly nutritious amaranth seeds in a gruel.

BEANS
These were part of the staple diet in both regions.

Fresh red and green chile peppers

Squash is related to the pumpkin

SQUASH
Squashes were cooked in stews.

Green tomato

Red tomato

TOMATOES
Tomatoes were a very important crop in Mesoamerica.

Vanilla pod

Vanilla was used for flavoring drinks

Dried chile peppers

VANILLA
Vanilla was a highly valued spice in Mesoamerica.

PEANUTS
A good source of protein, peanuts were grown and eaten in both regions.

CHILE PEPPERS
Hot chile peppers, both fresh and dried, were and still are common in both Mesoamerica and South America. Chiles were used as spices in all types of cooking.

Sweet potato

White potato

White corn

POTATO
Potatoes are native plants of the Andean region and were a central part of the diet. The Andean people grew many varieties.

PEPPERS
In addition to chiles, peppers that were not hot and spicy were also popular throughout Mesoamerica.

Black corn

CORN
Corn was the most important food of Mesoamerica. Along with the potato, it was a major crop in the Andes.

OCTLI **SUCKER**
The Aztecs had an alcoholic drink called *octli*, made from the fermented sap of the maguey (agave) plant. The sap was sucked from the plant (above).

Prickly pear

AVOCADO
The avocado fruit was widely eaten in Mesoamerica.

Toltec pot has turkey's head handle

CACTUS LEAVES
These leaves were peeled, boiled, and eaten with main dishes or on their own.

TURKEY
Turkey meat was considered a delicacy, along with dog meat.

PRICKLY PEAR
This is a sweet cactus fruit from Mesoamerica.

PUMPKIN
Pumpkins and squashes, along with corn and beans, were the staple foods in Mesoamerica.

Trade and tribute

CODEX TRIBUTE
In addition to dealing with history and daily life, the Aztec Codex Mendoza records details of tributes paid.

400 gourd bowls

400 simply decorated cotton blankets

400 heavily decorated cotton blankets

8,000 bundles of *copal* incense

60 jars of honey

2 containers, 1 of corn and 1 of chia seeds

IN MESOAMERICA and in the Andean region, it was the commoners who mainly supported the state by paying taxes. People of high rank did not pay taxes, nor did the sick and those with disabilities. In Inca territory, each province had to pay specific amounts of tribute to the government. At Tenochtitlan, the Aztec capital, the residents of each borough belonged to an institution called a *calpulli*, whose leader made sure that taxes were paid. Goods of all kinds were exchanged in both regions, and in Mesoamerica all the products of the land were sold in splendid marketplaces. Aztec merchants went on long expeditions to distant lands to trade for such items as tropical feathers, gold, fine stones, and jaguar skins.

RUNNER
This Moche pot depicts a runner. Runners, or *chasquis*, ran from one place to the next, usually carrying messages. The Incas had an excellent road system that was essential for controlling the empire, for trade, and for communication.

Jaguar headdress

THE SALE OF CORN
Much can be learned from the murals of Diego Rivera about how the ancient Mexicans lived. Rivera, one of the most remarkable modern Mexican muralists, was well-read about life in Tenochtitlan. This detail of a busy market scene shows women selling various types of corn.

WARRIOR'S SUIT AND SHIELD
Tunics and shields were very expensive items of tribute. Tunics were either made of feather-covered material or of animal pelts. The jaguar headdress (left) was one of the warrior's insignia and also a symbol of power. According to the Codex Mendoza, tribute of this kind had to be paid once a year.

Jaguar warrior's suit

Feather shield

FUR TRADE
Animal skins were sold in the market at Tlatelolco. The skin of the puma was particularly valued by the Maya, because its tawny color reminded them of the Sun. Jaguar skins were equally valued. Their black spots were thought to symbolize the night sky. Jaguar skins were used as seats for the rulers and as book covers. They were also worn as cloaks.

Ocelot skin

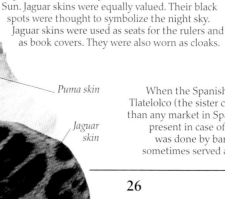

Puma skin

Jaguar skin

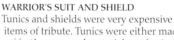

TLATELOLCO MARKET
When the Spanish arrived in Mexico, they found that the market at Tlatelolco (the sister city of Tenochtitlan) was bigger and better stocked than any market in Spain. Supervisors regulated prices, and judges were present in case of disputes or theft. Much of the buying and selling was done by barter—exchanging products—although copper axes sometimes served as money in both Mesoamerica and in the Andes.

Recording storehouse
goods on a *quipu*

Cocoa beans

Melon seeds

Ax
heads

Quetzal
feather

Jade beads

Tropical bird
feather

TRADING
Items such as cocoa beans and
feathers were in great demand,
since vast quantities of each were
paid in tribute. The merchants
from Tenochtitlan and
neighboring major cities
exported and traded luxury objects
made from imported raw materials
or materials obtained by tribute.
In return for their wares, they
obtained goods such as tropical
feathers (especially quetzal feathers),
cocoa beans, animal skins, and gold.

Storing agricultural produce
in government granaries

INCAN STOREHOUSES *left*
The Incas stockpiled goods such as cloth,
corn, wool, potatoes, and weapons in
storehouses. These supplies could be used
by government officials and those who
were in need due to an illness. They could
also be distributed after a crisis or a siege.

*Simply decorated pottery
vessel for everyday use*

*All the pottery stalls
were placed together
in the market*

Simple pottery bowl

*People met at the
market to exchange
news as well as goods*

The warrior

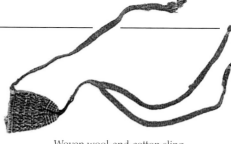

WARFARE was a normal part of life in both Mesoamerica and the Incan region of South America, and city-states frequently fought each other. In Mesoamerica, youths had to join the army at the age of 17 for a period of intensive training. The Incan and Mesoamerican peoples were educated in the arts of war, and the fighting spirit was encouraged. Among the Aztecs, the best and most common way to climb the social ladder was by showing courage in battle. One of the main goals of going to war was to capture enemy warriors for sacrifice. Aztec warriors were in a constant "sacred war," since they believed that human sacrifice kept the Sun in motion (pp. 36–37). Both the Incas and the Aztecs added newly conquered areas to their empires. As power and wealth grew, they developed a thirst for more conquests that would enrich the state and add to the glory of the emperor.

Woven wool-and-cotton sling, used by a Peruvian Chancay warrior to hurl stones at enemies

TOLTEC WARRIOR
This sculpture shows a richly attired Toltec warrior wearing a feather headdress, ear plugs, and a butterfly breastplate. In one hand he carries an *atlatl*, or spear thrower, and in the other a sheaf of darts.

CAPTURED
For taking captives, Aztec warriors were awarded costumes with distinctive designs, such as jaguar costumes and mantles. The more captives a warrior took, the more elaborate his costume.

Flint knife has a sharp serrated edge

AZTEC WEAPONS
A warrior usually carried one or two throwing spears. They were made of wood and edged with obsidian—a volcanic glass that is sharp enough to sever a horse's head—or a type of stone called chert. He also had a wooden *macuahuitl*, or war club, edged with obsidian. In addition to a club and spears, warriors carried stabbing javelins and round shields with protective feather fringes. Flint and obsidian knives (left) were also used for human sacrifices.

Club

Long, razor-sharp knife made from obsidian

WAR CLUB
The *macuahuitl*, or war club, was about 30 in (76 cm) long. It had grooved sides set with sharp obsidian blades.

EFFIGY POT
The Moche culture from the north coast of Peru often depicted warriors on pottery vessels, such as this warrior holding a club. Shields were often shown strapped to the wrists.

THROWING SPEAR
The flakes of sharp obsidian stone around the head of a wooden throwing spear were capable of inflicting deep cuts.

Obsidian blades around head of spear

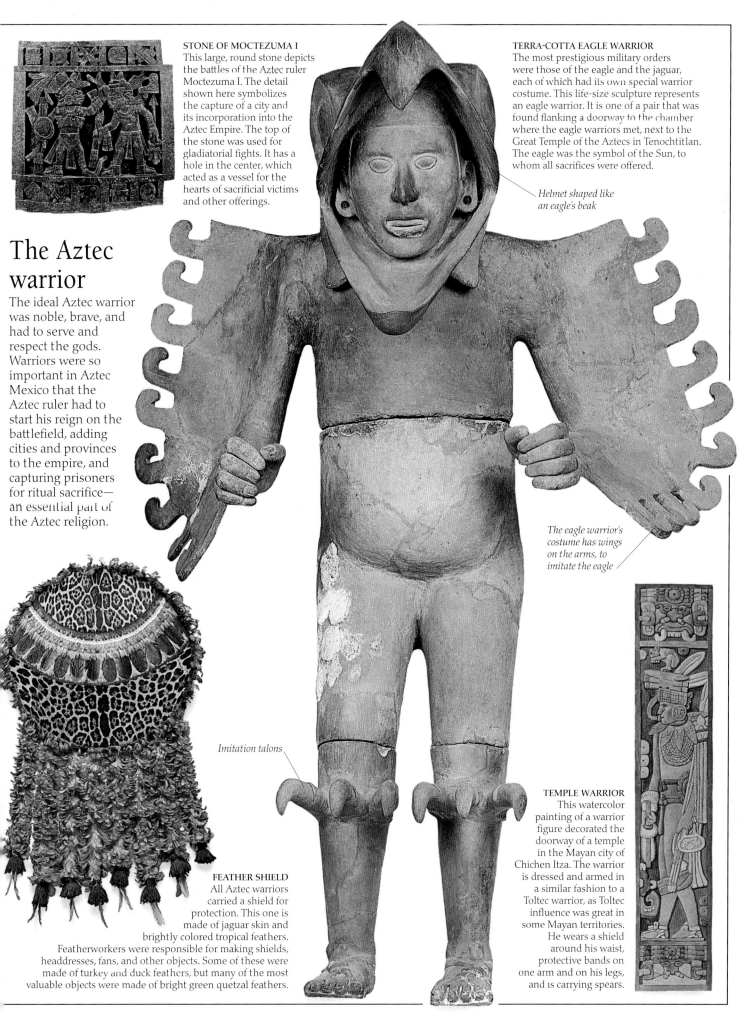

This large, round stone depicts the battles of the Aztec ruler Moctezuma I. The detail shown here symbolizes the capture of a city and its incorporation into the Aztec Empire. The top of the stone was used for gladiatorial fights. It has a hole in the center, which acted as a vessel for the hearts of sacrificial victims and other offerings.

TERRA-COTTA EAGLE WARRIOR
The most prestigious military orders were those of the eagle and the jaguar, each of which had its own special warrior costume. This life-size sculpture represents an eagle warrior. It is one of a pair that was found flanking a doorway to the chamber where the eagle warriors met, next to the Great Temple of the Aztecs in Tenochtitlan. The eagle was the symbol of the Sun, to whom all sacrifices were offered.

Helmet shaped like an eagle's beak

The Aztec warrior

The ideal Aztec warrior was noble, brave, and had to serve and respect the gods. Warriors were so important in Aztec Mexico that the Aztec ruler had to start his reign on the battlefield, adding cities and provinces to the empire, and capturing prisoners for ritual sacrifice—an essential part of the Aztec religion.

The eagle warrior's costume has wings on the arms, to imitate the eagle

Imitation talons

FEATHER SHIELD
All Aztec warriors carried a shield for protection. This one is made of jaguar skin and brightly colored tropical feathers. Featherworkers were responsible for making shields, headdresses, fans, and other objects. Some of these were made of turkey and duck feathers, but many of the most valuable objects were made of bright green quetzal feathers.

TEMPLE WARRIOR
This watercolor painting of a warrior figure decorated the doorway of a temple in the Mayan city of Chichen Itza. The warrior is dressed and armed in a similar fashion to a Toltec warrior, as Toltec influence was great in some Mayan territories. He wears a shield around his waist, protective bands on one arm and on his legs, and is carrying spears.

Religious life

RELIGION TOUCHED almost every aspect of Mesoamerican and Incan life. One of the many focal points for their religious rites were sacred buildings, or temples, dedicated to their gods.

In the Andean region, everyone worshiped a variety of shrines and objects and the natural forces associated with them, known as *huacas*. The Aztecs also worshiped sacred places. Within the official Incan state religion the Sun was the most important god. It was a dominant force and a symbol of prestige and power. The Incas worshiped the Sun mainly so that they would have abundant crops. The Aztec religion was also concerned with the Sun. The Aztecs believed that they lived in the era of the fifth Sun and that one day the world would end violently. In order to postpone their destruction, men performed human sacrifices. Their duty was to feed the gods with human blood, thereby keeping the Sun alive.

Codex illustration of an Aztec temple at Tenochtitlan

TEMPLE OF THE GIANT JAGUAR
To worship their gods, the Maya built magnificent ceremonial centers filled with temples, courts, and plazas. This majestic temple stands in the ceremonial center of the Mayan city of Tikal. Also known as Temple I, it is the funerary pyramid of the Mayan ruler Hasaw Chan K'awil. It has nine sloping terraces and is topped by a huge ornamental structure called a roof comb.

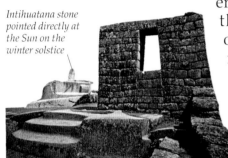

Intihuatana stone pointed directly at the Sun on the winter solstice

SOLSTICE STONE
Throughout their empire, the Incas built temples for the cult of the Sun. The Intihuatana stone at Machu Picchu worked as a solar clock. It allowed people to calculate the winter solstice for the important festival of the Sun god. Intihuatana means "hitching post of the Sun."

Priests performing rituals in New Fire ceremony

Bodies of sacrificial victims thrown down stairs after sacrifice

AZTEC NEW FIRE CEREMONY
This religious event took place in temples every 52 years. When the day arrived, people extinguished all fires and discarded idols and household utensils. The new century began when the Sun's rays appeared again at dawn.

MODEL OF THE GREAT TEMPLE AT TENOCHTITLAN
At the heart of the city of Tenochtitlan was a walled precinct. Within it, sharing a single tall pyramid, were the twin shrines to Tlaloc, the god of rain, and Huitzilopochtli, the god of war and the tribal god of the Aztecs. The Great Temple was the physical and symbolic center of the Aztec world, where human sacrifices and offerings to the gods took place. Each Aztec ruler tried to make a bigger and more impressive new temple. This model shows the many temples that were built, one above the other. The oldest, inner temple has a *chacmool* (a sculpture with a receptacle for hearts and blood) on the left and a sacrificial stone on the right. The excavators of the site found more than 6,000 objects buried as offerings to Tlaloc and Huitzilopochtli.

Shrine to Tlaloc, god of rain

Chacmool

Shrine to Huitzilopochtli, god of war

Sacrificial stone

SKULL PANEL
Real skulls were placed outside temples in skull racks, known in the Aztec language of Nahautl as *tzompantli*. This panel of skulls is from the Great Temple of the Aztecs. The skulls were usually those of people sacrificed to the gods.

Sculpture still has traces of its original paintwork

RECLINING FIGURE
This *chacmool* was found at the entrance of the shrine to Tlaloc at the summit of the Great Temple of Tenochtitlan. He holds a container for the hearts and blood of people sacrificed to the gods of rain and agriculture.

Snake's head protruding from wall

Gods and goddesses

Yacatecuhtli, Aztec god of merchants and travelers

THE MESOAMERICAN and Incan peoples worshiped many gods. They had similar religions—based on the worship of mainly agricultural gods—even though the gods' names and the symbols for them were different. People asked their gods for good crops and good health. The main Incan god was the creator god Viracocha. His assistants were the gods of the Sun, Moon, stars, and thunder, as well as the gods of the Earth and the sea. Since farming occupied such an important place in both regions, the "Earth mother," or Earth goddess, was particularly important. As with Incan deities, many Aztec gods were connected with nature or natural forces, but the Aztecs also had other gods, including gods of war, hunting, and merchants.

Xipe Totec wearing the skin of a sacrificial victim

RAIN GOD
Many Mesoamerican vessels and sculptures are associated with Tlaloc, the god of rain and agricultural fertility. It is likely that this water vessel depicts the face of the god of rain, since it contains the vital liquid necessary to fertilize the soil.

Tlaloc had "goggle eyes"

GOD OF THE SPRINGTIME
The Aztec god of the springtime and of vegetation was named Xipe Totec ("Our Flayed Lord"). He was also the patron of metal workers. The victims sacrificed in honor of this god were flayed (skinned alive). After flaying the victim, priests would wear his skin. This symbolized the annual spring renewal of vegetation—in other words, the renewal of the Earth's "skin."

Xipe Totec, god of springtime and of vegetation

Quetzalcoatl, the feathered serpent

Tlaloc, the rain god

Reconstruction of temple of Quetzalcoatl in Teotihuacan

GOD OF NATURE
Quetzalcoatl, whose name means "feathered serpent," was a god of nature—of the air and the Earth. The temple of Quetzalcoatl at Teotihuacan is decorated with large sculptures of feathered serpents, as this reconstruction shows.

Chicomecoatl wore a rectangular headdress with pleated rosettes at the corners

AZTEC CORN GODDESS
Three goddesses were associated with corn. This statue depicts Chicomecoatl, the goddess of mature corn. This was the best seed-corn of the harvest, which was put away for sowing. There was also a goddess of tender corn and another who was the personification of the corn plant.

Double corncobs

The Incas worshiped the Moon and the Sun

SEPTEMBER FESTIVAL
The Incas celebrated different religious festivities each month of the year. Here we see the celebrations for September, which were dedicated to female goddesses. This festivity was celebrated under the protection of the Moon and the Sun gods.

WAR GOD
Huitzilopochtli ("The Hummingbird of the Left") was the tribal god of the Aztecs. This illustration shows him armed with his serpent of fire and his shield.

GOD OF THE DEAD
Mictlantecuhtli was god of the dead in Aztec Mexico. Those who died a natural death went to Mictlan, the place where he lived, in the cold and infernal region of the fleshless.

WORSHIPING THE SUN
Worship of Inti, the Sun god, was pivotal to Incan religion. Both Aztecs and Incas worshiped the Sun and the Earth, Mamachocha ("Mother of the lakes and sea"), which are both essential for good harvests. The Sun was the most important god of the Incan royal dynasty. Incan kings believed that they were descendants of Inti.

Gold disk

SKY OR MOON GOD
The handle of this Peruvian ceremonial knife is decorated with the image of either the sky or the Moon god. His arms are opened wide, and he is holding two disks. He wears a beautiful filigree headdress with turquoise inlay.

Turquoise was used for the inlays of the eyes, necklace, ear plugs, and the clothing

Ornate ceremonial knife handle

Ceremonial urn depicting Chac with a bowl in his right hand and a ball of smoking incense in his left

MAYAN GOD OF RAIN
The Mayan god of rain was named Chac. One of the sacrifices in honor of this god was to drown children in wells. In some regions, the god of rain was so important that the facades of buildings were covered with masks of Chac.

Life after death

THE PEOPLE OF Mesoamerica and South America believed that, after they died, they would carry on living in another world. They were buried with all kinds of things that might prove useful to them in the afterlife. By studying the goods found in graves, pre-Hispanic codices, and early colonial manuscripts, archeologists have pieced together some of their beliefs about death and the afterlife. It was the way the Aztecs died, rather than the way they lived, that decided what would happen to them in the afterlife. If a person died a normal death, his or her soul had to pass through the nine levels of the underworld before reaching Mictlan, the realm of the god of the dead. Warriors who died in battle and women who died in childbirth went to join the Sun god in the sky.

Chancay "doll" found in grave

DOLL COMPANION
Colorful figures found in Chancay tombs, such as this one, are called "dolls" because it is believed that they were used in daily life. They were placed with the deceased to serve them in the afterlife.

MUMMY OF DEAD KING
In Andean society, mummies were looked after as if they were alive. The living often consulted the dead about important matters. At special festivals, the mummies of emperors were paraded in the streets.

ALL WRAPPED UP
Many mummy bundles have been discovered in the Andean region. The corpse was placed in a flexed position and bound with cord to help maintain the pose. It was then wrapped in textiles and seated upright. Goods were placed around the mummy in the grave.

Mayan child's burial urn

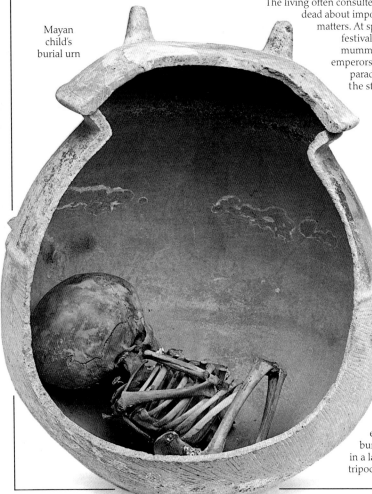

THE RICH AND THE POOR
The more goods that were placed in a grave, the better off the individual was. Wooden figurines, such as this one of a man, have been found in many Andean tombs. But tombs filled with golden objects, and where the corpse has been more elaborately prepared, indicate that everyone was not equal.

MAYAN BURIAL
The Maya usually buried their dead under house floors or in the ground. Sometimes, however, they cremated the remains or buried them in caves, underground tanks, or urns. The privileged classes were buried in very elaborate tombs. One common type of burial for children was to place the corpse in a large urn, which was then covered by a tripod (three-legged) vessel or pot fragment.

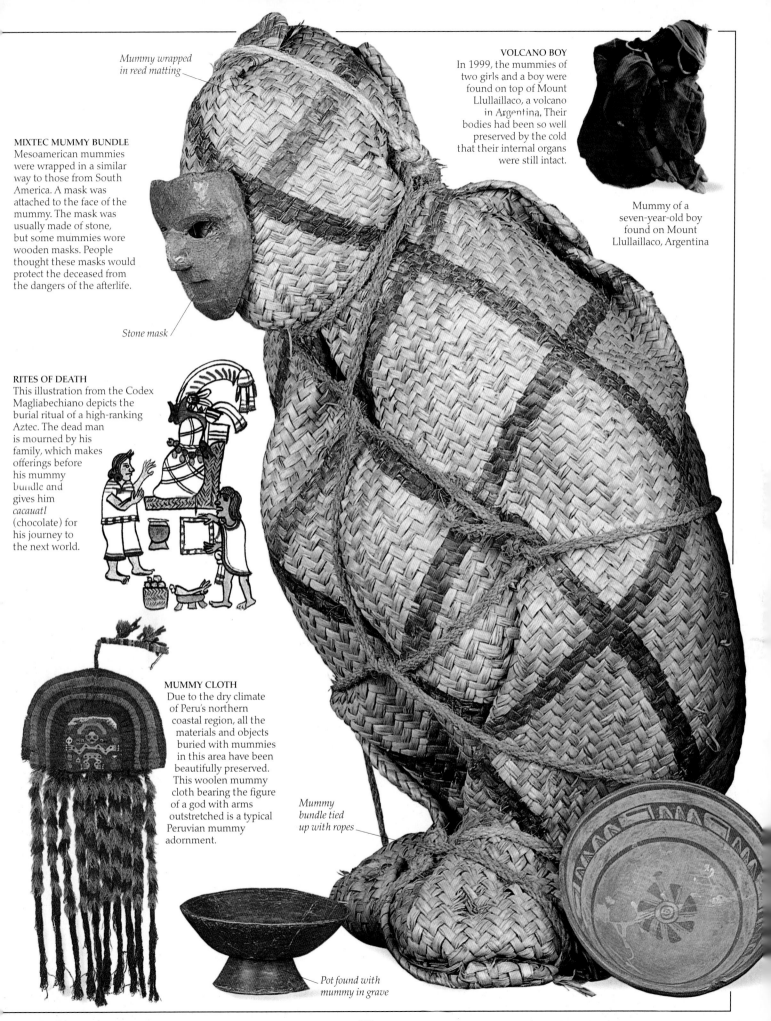

Mummy wrapped in reed matting

MIXTEC MUMMY BUNDLE
Mesoamerican mummies were wrapped in a similar way to those from South America. A mask was attached to the face of the mummy. The mask was usually made of stone, but some mummies wore wooden masks. People thought these masks would protect the deceased from the dangers of the afterlife.

Stone mask

VOLCANO BOY
In 1999, the mummies of two girls and a boy were found on top of Mount Llullaillaco, a volcano in Argentina, Their bodies had been so well preserved by the cold that their internal organs were still intact.

Mummy of a seven-year-old boy found on Mount Llullaillaco, Argentina

RITES OF DEATH
This illustration from the Codex Magliabechiano depicts the burial ritual of a high-ranking Aztec. The dead man is mourned by his family, which makes offerings before his mummy bundle and gives him *cacauatl* (chocolate) for his journey to the next world.

MUMMY CLOTH
Due to the dry climate of Peru's northern coastal region, all the materials and objects buried with mummies in this area have been beautifully preserved. This woolen mummy cloth bearing the figure of a god with arms outstretched is a typical Peruvian mummy adornment.

Mummy bundle tied up with ropes

Pot found with mummy in grave

Human sacrifice

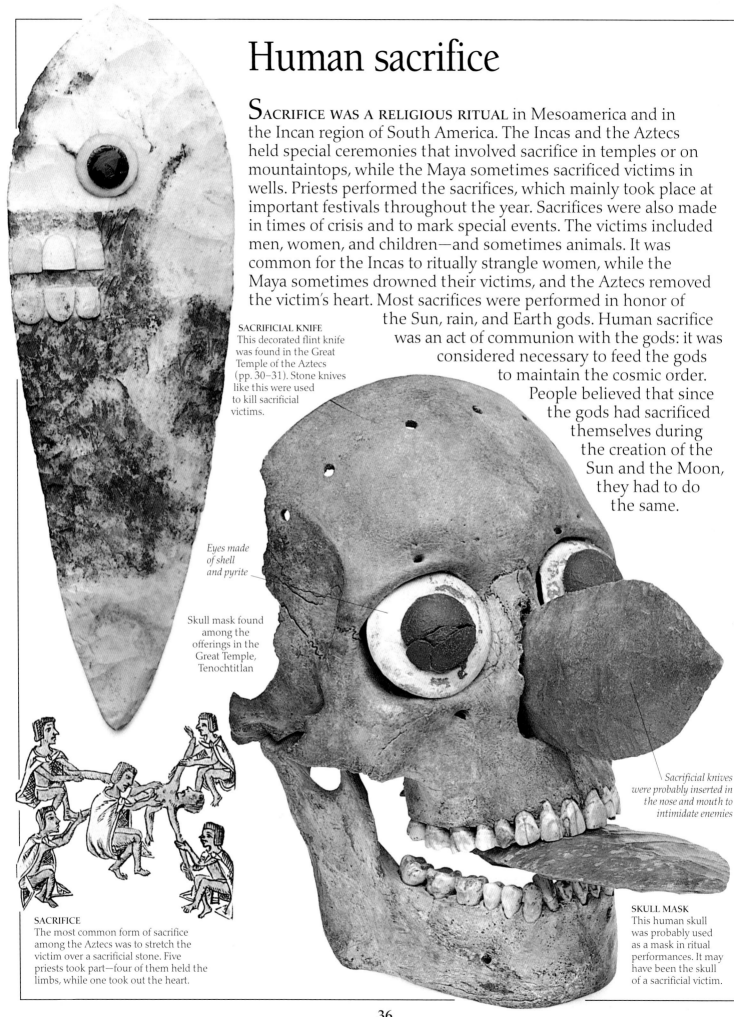

SACRIFICE WAS A RELIGIOUS RITUAL in Mesoamerica and in the Incan region of South America. The Incas and the Aztecs held special ceremonies that involved sacrifice in temples or on mountaintops, while the Maya sometimes sacrificed victims in wells. Priests performed the sacrifices, which mainly took place at important festivals throughout the year. Sacrifices were also made in times of crisis and to mark special events. The victims included men, women, and children—and sometimes animals. It was common for the Incas to ritually strangle women, while the Maya sometimes drowned their victims, and the Aztecs removed the victim's heart. Most sacrifices were performed in honor of the Sun, rain, and Earth gods. Human sacrifice was an act of communion with the gods: it was considered necessary to feed the gods to maintain the cosmic order. People believed that since the gods had sacrificed themselves during the creation of the Sun and the Moon, they had to do the same.

SACRIFICIAL KNIFE
This decorated flint knife was found in the Great Temple of the Aztecs (pp. 30–31). Stone knives like this were used to kill sacrificial victims.

Eyes made of shell and pyrite

Skull mask found among the offerings in the Great Temple, Tenochtitlan

Sacrificial knives were probably inserted in the nose and mouth to intimidate enemies

SACRIFICE
The most common form of sacrifice among the Aztecs was to stretch the victim over a sacrificial stone. Five priests took part—four of them held the limbs, while one took out the heart.

SKULL MASK
This human skull was probably used as a mask in ritual performances. It may have been the skull of a sacrificial victim.

AFTER SACRIFICE
Once an Aztec priest had taken the heart out, it was placed in a receptacle like the one below. The victim was then thrown down the temple stairs. The body was picked up and part of it, such as the thigh, was given as a reward to the victim's captor. The Aztecs practiced cannibalism in some religious ceremonies under strict regulations. For example, enemy captives were ritually eaten, but only legs or arms could be consumed.

Illustration from Codex Magliabecchiano

The skull symbol often appears in Aztec art

PRECIOUS HEART
This beautifully carved greenstone heart represents the most precious organ that the Aztecs could offer to their gods. Likewise, jade was considered the most valuable stone and the most precious material, far more so than gold. Jade was the symbol of life and agriculture.

SACRIFICIAL STONES AND VESSELS
This ritual vessel (right) may have been intended to contain the blood or the hearts of sacrificial victims. The outer surface is decorated with skulls. The skull was a symbol of fame, glory, or defeat, depending on the situation. The stone below is one kind of stone that was used for the act of sacrifice. The victim would have been stretched over this stone while having his or her heart plucked out.

Ritual vessel

Sacrificial stone

MOUNTAINTOP SACRIFICE
The tops of high mountains and volcanoes were sacred places. Here people worshiped the Earth gods, who were the providers of water and agriculture, and made human sacrifices to them. Water was considered to be the blood of agricultural life. Human sacrifices were performed for many reasons. They were generally considered a present to the gods in exchange for a favor requested—such as a good harvest. Those who were sacrificed were thought to be fortunate, since they were guaranteed a life of ease in the world to come.

Ornate Moche water pot depicting men sitting high up in the mountain peaks

FLAYED ALIVE
This 19th-century illustration shows human sacrifice by flaying, or skinning a man alive. The ancient Peruvians performed this kind of ritual sacrifice. Skinning was also practiced by the ancient Mexicans during agricultural festivities. Like the ancient Mexicans, the ancient Peruvians had many sacrificial victims dedicated to the Sun, Inti, or to the creator god, Viracocha.

Medicine

Snakeroot, taken for stomach pains

Pudding pipe-tree, a laxative, taken for coughs and fever

IN MESOAMERICA and in the Andean cultures, treatments for illnesses were a mixture of magic and knowledge of the body. Mesoamerican midwives, healers, and physicians were often women who were well versed in the use of herbs. The Andeans believed that disease had a supernatural cause. They treated the sick with herbs for both magical and medicinal reasons. The Aztecs used certain minerals for medicine, as well as the flesh of some animals. The Incas used urine for treating fever, and often bled themselves. Inca surgeons bored holes in the skull and amputated limbs when necessary. Both Mesoamericans and Andeans used obsidian knives and lancets for surgery.

Drinking a herbal infusion to treat fever

MEDICINE SELECTION
Various plants and herbs were used as medicine. The rabbit fern root was taken as a remedy for rheumatism and to treat bites by poisonous animals. Some roots were particularly useful for treating kidney complaints, and palm nuts were taken for circulation ailments. Despite its bitter taste, quinine (from the bark of a Peruvian tree) was taken to prevent and treat malaria.

Rabbit fern, taken for rheumatism

Palm nuts, taken for circulation problems

Quinine, taken for malaria

BANDAGING A LEG
Physicians had a good knowledge of the body, and they were often right in their diagnoses. This Aztec surgeon is bandaging an injured leg.

MAN SUFFERING FROM TUBERCULOSIS
Like the Andeans, the Aztecs also portrayed diseases and deformities in their art. This sculpture is of a man suffering from tuberculosis, one of the most serious ailments in ancient Mexico. Tuberculosis afflicted many young people. The realism of the sculpture allows us to see the deformed back caused by the disease.

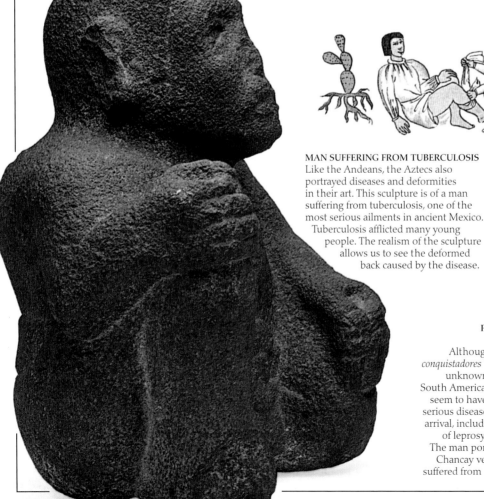

POTTERY MAN WITH SPOTS
Although the Spanish *conquistadores* brought many unknown diseases into South America, the Andeans seem to have known some serious diseases before their arrival, including *uta* (a type of leprosy) and syphilis. The man portrayed on this Chancay vessel may have suffered from either disease.

Peyote cactus

Peyote has long roots

CACTUS TOPS

Some plants and seeds, such as *ololiuhqui* (Morning glory) seeds, were taken by the ancient Mexicans as medicines. Along with the tops of the peyote cactus (above) from northern Mexico, these seeds were also widely taken as drugs. People who ate them experienced colorful hallucinations. Drugs that caused hallucinations were also consumed in order for people to communicate with the gods.

MARKET MEDICINE STALL

In Mesoamerica, wild plants and herbs were cultivated in botanical gardens for medicinal purposes and sold in markets. There were roots, seeds, maguey leaves, *copal* resin, and many other types of plant for treating a range of ailments, from snake bites to gout and fever. The ancient Mexicans believed that *copal* smoke cured diseases. Tobacco powder was inhaled by the Andeans to help clear the head, but in Mesoamerica it was also smoked for pleasure. Many seeds and roots were combined with vanilla, cocoa, and corn to make the medicine more palatable, although many of these flavorings were considered medicinal in their own right.

Snakeskins and snake flesh were taken for various illnesses

Nuts and seeds

Leaves and roots

Writing and counting

ANCIENT AZTEC GODS
According to Aztec mythology, the most ancient gods and the creators of the universe were "Lord and Lady of our Austenance." They are associated with time and the calendar.

Knotted strings hang from horizontal cord

BOTH THE MESOAMERICAN PEOPLE and the ancient Peruvians kept records. However, what they recorded and how they did this was very different. Mesoamerican cultures had a picture-writing system and kept details of their history and administration, while the Peruvians had no written records. The Incas recorded information about tribute (p. 27) and goods in storage on an arrangement of knotted strings called a *quipu*. Many Mesoamerican pictures (or glyphs) were pictograms, in which an object or an idea was represented by a drawing—for example, a shield and a club signified war. This type of writing was kept in books called codices, painted on walls and vases, and carved into a variety of objects, from stone monuments to tiny pieces of jade.

The Mesoamericans were obsessed by counting and the passage of time. Both the Aztecs and the Maya devised a vegisimal counting system (based on units of 20), and they had two calendars—the solar calendar and the sacred almanac.

HIGH SOCIETY
Only the elite, a small fraction of Mesoamerican society, could read and interpret written records. This Mayan woman is reading a book on her knee.

AZTEC DAYS OF THE MONTH
The Aztec solar calendar year was 365 days long. It consisted of 18 months of 20 days and five extra days that were thought to be unlucky. This illustration shows four days of the month—flint knife, rain, flower, and alligator.

MAYAN PAINTED BOOK
Codices were made of paper, cloth made from fibers of the maguey plant, or animal skin. There are four Mayan codices in existence. This one, the Codex Tro-Cortesianus, contains information about divination (predicting the future) and rituals for Mayan priests. Mayan codices were written or painted with fine brushes onto long strips of bark paper that were covered with a layer of chalky paste (gesso) and folded like screens.

Numbers recorded with knots of varying sizes

INCA ACCOUNTANT
A special accountant was in charge of keeping records. He was skilled in recording figures, whether of people, llamas, or what tribute was to be paid.

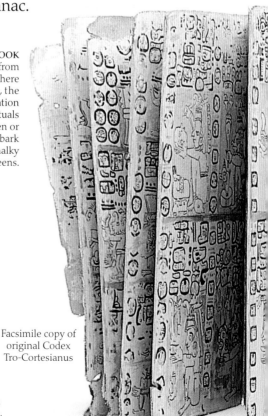

Facsimile copy of original Codex Tro-Cortesianus

INCA COUNTING DEVICE
The *quipu* was a length of cord held horizontally, from which hung knotted strings of various thicknesses and colors. The information recorded varied according to the types of knots, the cord's length, and the color and position of the strings. The *quipu* was probably used to record the census and for taxation purposes.

AZTEC SUN STONE

This stone is one of the largest Aztec sculptures ever found, measuring about 13 ft (4 m) in diameter. At the center of the stone is the face of the Sun, or that of the Lord of the Earth. This carving is sometimes called the Calendar Stone, but it actually represents the Aztec belief that the universe had already passed through four world creations, which had all been destroyed. We are now in the fifth creation, which is doomed to be destroyed by earthquakes. According to Aztec mythology, the Sun, the Moon, and human beings were successfully created at the beginning of the fifth era.

Sun, or Lord of the Earth

One of the previous four world creations

This band shows the 20 days of the month

The date glyph on this sculpture is "day one death"

RIDDLE OF THE GLYPHS

The study of Mayan hieroglyphic writing began in 1827. By 1950, names of gods and animals had been identified. In 1960, researchers realized that Mayan inscriptions were primarily historical. They deal with the births, accessions, wars, deaths, and marriages of Mayan kings. This Mayan stone carving was placed over doors and windows. It has a glyph that dates it to the 6th century CE.

BUNDLE OF YEARS

The Aztecs divided time into "centuries" of 52 years. At the end of each cycle and the beginning of a new one, an Aztec ceremony called "the binding of the years" took place. In sculpture, each cycle is represented by a bundle of reeds accompanied by dates. This sculpted stone bundle symbolizes the death of an Aztec century.

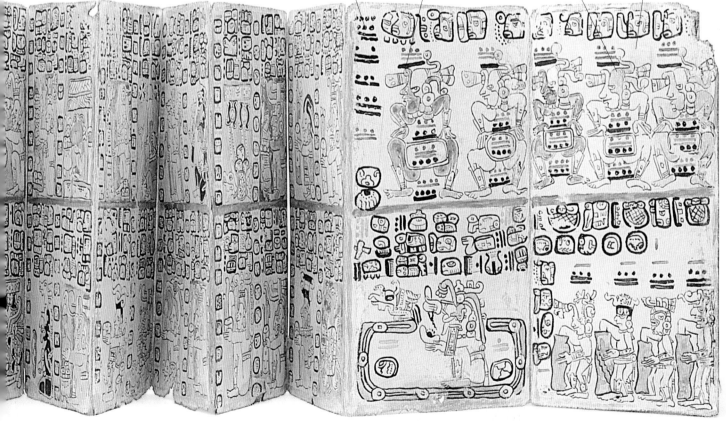

Bars and dots are Mayan glyphs for numbers

Codex was read from top to bottom, and from left to right

Glyphs showing five gods

Fine layer of gesso (chalky paste)

Weaving and spinning

Nazca textile with fringed border

Andean woman weaving on a back-strap loom

N<small>O OTHER PEOPLE</small> in the Americas left such a wealth of marvelous woven textiles as the ancient Peruvians. Their exquisitely worked textiles have survived in graves in desertlike areas of Peru. The tradition of weaving and spinning was practiced by all women, both in Mesoamerica and in the Andean region. They were expected to spin and weave for their families' needs, and also provide woven goods for payment of tribute and taxes to their rulers. Textiles were woven mainly from cotton and maguey fiber in Mesoamerica, while alpaca and llama wool were widely used in the Andean region.

NATURAL DYES
In Mesoamerica, cotton was used for making textiles for the upper classes; maguey, yucca, and other fibers were woven for the commoners. The yarn was dyed before it was woven. Some dyes were made from the juice of flowers and fruits, but dyes were also extracted from shellfish and from the cochineal—a tiny insect that lives on the cactus plant.

Loom bar, attached to a tree or post

Long threads fixed to the loom bars are called the warp

Shed rod

BACK-STRAP LOOM
The most common loom used in the Americas was the back-strap loom. It is still widely used today. The loom consists of two loom bars, which are poles that hold the warp (vertical) threads. One bar is hooked to a support such as a tree or post, while the other is secured by a belt around the weaver's back. When the warp is stretched taut, the weft (horizontal) thread is passed under and over the strands of the warp using a heddle stick and a shed rod to lift up alternate strands. To alter the pattern or introduce more color, more heddles are used, or different groups of warp threads are lifted up.

Heddle stick grasped with left hand

Weaving sword used to smooth down weft threads

Weft threads run alternately under and over warp threads

Figurine may be of Mayan goddess Ixchel, patroness of weaving

Back-strap loom

Strap fit around weaver's waist

MAYAN LADY WEAVING
This Mayan figurine shows a young lady sitting on the ground, weaving with a back-strap loom.

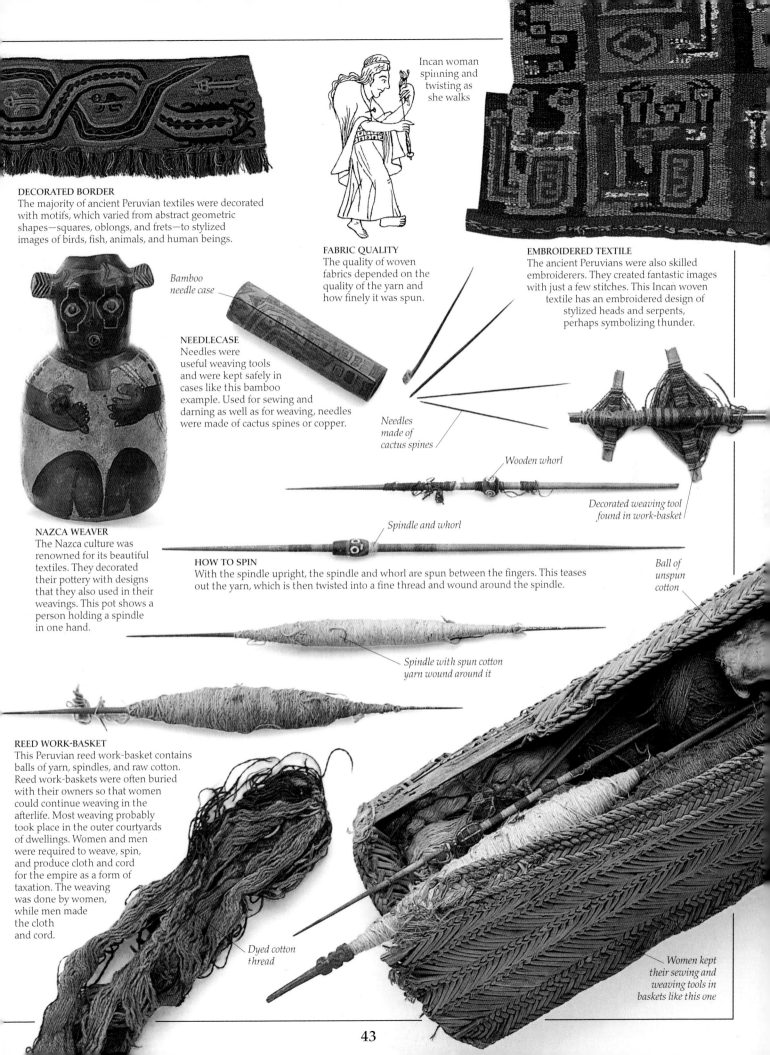

DECORATED BORDER
The majority of ancient Peruvian textiles were decorated with motifs, which varied from abstract geometric shapes—squares, oblongs, and frets—to stylized images of birds, fish, animals, and human beings.

Incan woman spinning and twisting as she walks

Bamboo needle case

NEEDLECASE
Needles were useful weaving tools and were kept safely in cases like this bamboo example. Used for sewing and darning as well as for weaving, needles were made of cactus spines or copper.

FABRIC QUALITY
The quality of woven fabrics depended on the quality of the yarn and how finely it was spun.

EMBROIDERED TEXTILE
The ancient Peruvians were also skilled embroiderers. They created fantastic images with just a few stitches. This Incan woven textile has an embroidered design of stylized heads and serpents, perhaps symbolizing thunder.

Needles made of cactus spines

Wooden whorl

Decorated weaving tool found in work-basket

Spindle and whorl

NAZCA WEAVER
The Nazca culture was renowned for its beautiful textiles. They decorated their pottery with designs that they also used in their weavings. This pot shows a person holding a spindle in one hand.

HOW TO SPIN
With the spindle upright, the spindle and whorl are spun between the fingers. This teases out the yarn, which is then twisted into a fine thread and wound around the spindle.

Ball of unspun cotton

Spindle with spun cotton yarn wound around it

REED WORK-BASKET
This Peruvian reed work-basket contains balls of yarn, spindles, and raw cotton. Reed work-baskets were often buried with their owners so that women could continue weaving in the afterlife. Most weaving probably took place in the outer courtyards of dwellings. Women and men were required to weave, spin, and produce cloth and cord for the empire as a form of taxation. The weaving was done by women, while men made the cloth and cord.

Dyed cotton thread

Women kept their sewing and weaving tools in baskets like this one

Clothes and accessories

CLOTHING STYLES WERE VERY DIFFERENT in Mesoamerica and South America, but in both regions they reflected a person's social class. People who wore clothes made of fine material with colorful and elaborate decoration were of high status. The Incas made their clothes mainly from wool, although on the coast cotton was preferred. Ordinary people wore alpaca-wool garments; silky vicuña wool was worn by the nobles. Mesoamerican clothes were made from cotton or other plant fibers. All items of clothing were very simple. Many were just a piece of material draped around a part of the body. Men from both regions wore loincloths. Aztec women wore a skirt wrapped around the hips, and men wore cloaks draped over the shoulder. Ponchos and tunics slipped over the head and were sewn at the sides.

CAPPING IT ALL
In the Andean region, people wore knitted wool or cotton caps. This handsome Chimu woolen cap with colorful panels is unusual, being woven, not knitted.

SANDAL
The Incas made sandals with leather from the neck of the llama. In other regions, sandals were made of wool or, as in this case, the fiber of the aloe plant.

Braided wool fastening

IN THE BAG
All Peruvian men carried a small bag under their cloaks, slung over the shoulder. In it they carried *coca* leaves for chewing and amulets (good-luck charms).

SLEEVELESS PONCHO *right*
Some ponchos were decorated with fine patterns. They were such important garments that the dead were buried with ponchos. In the highland regions of Peru, both men and women still wear ponchos today.

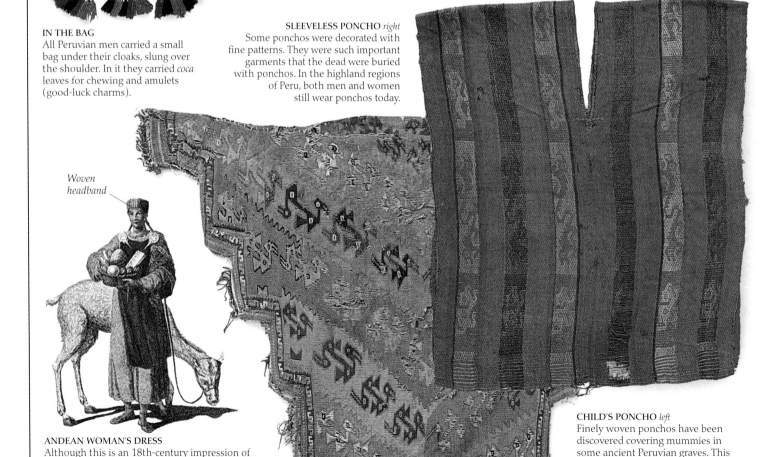

Woven headband

ANDEAN WOMAN'S DRESS
Although this is an 18th-century impression of a Peruvian woman, her clothing is similar to that worn by an Incan woman: a long dress of woven rectangular cloth, with a long cloak and sandals.

CHILD'S PONCHO *left*
Finely woven ponchos have been discovered covering mummies in some ancient Peruvian graves. This small poncho was found in a child's grave. It is woven from wool, with a design of birds in diagonal bands.

SHELL NECKLACE
In Mesoamerica, only the ruler and nobles could wear jewelry such as headbands, armbands, or nose, lip, and ear plugs. Even necklaces made of shells, like this one, could not be worn by everyone.

DIFFERENT CLOTHES, DIFFERENT JOBS
Aztec people wore clothes that suited their role in society. The lavish headdresses and rich materials worn here show that these are people of high rank.

COORDINATED CLOTHES
This Mayan woman is wearing a matching turban, skirt, and shawl. Her beautiful long hair is tied back with white ribbons. She wears a feather ornament in one ear and a bracelet that is probably made of leather.

Parasol

Elaborate headdress with two folds

SOPHISTICATED LADY
This richly attired figure is obviously a high-ranking Mayan woman. She wears a headdress with two folds and blue ear plugs that perhaps represent turquoise. Her beaded necklace is similar in shape to Mayan jade necklaces, and she wears bracelets on both arms. With one hand she protects her face with a parasol.

FANCY CAPE
Capes like this one were worn throughout Mesoamerica. This army commander is of a high rank, so his cape is finely decorated.

Robe with holes for arms and square-cut neck

MALE FASHION
This life-sized head of a Mixtec man shows what adornments they wore. He has a headband tied around his forehead, with a bird's head at the center and blue disks at the sides. His hair is loose, and he wears round blue ear plugs. His mouth is painted with black and white spots, resembling a mouth ornament.

Mayan women often walked barefoot

MAYAN FRESCO VASE
The cylindrical pot, such as this one decorated with a jaguar figure, was a common form of Mayan pottery. It was covered with stucco (plaster) and painted over while still wet.

Master potters

THE DECORATED CERAMICS of ancient Andean cultures are one of their most striking achievements. The Mesoamericans also had a rich and varied pottery tradition. Potters did not use a potter's wheel in either region. They produced a wide range of shapes, which they painted, carved, or stamped for decoration. The finest ceramics were for the rich or for ritual use. Pottery for everyday use was more simple. Because the Andean cultures had no writing system, pottery is a valuable source of information about the societies who made it, their religious ideas, and cultural influences.

ARYBALLUS JAR
Incan pottery was of excellent quality and was made in a few standard shapes. The most typical was the aryballus jar, with a conical base and a tall, flaring neck.

Jar used for storing water or possibly chicha beer

STIRRUP-SPOUTED MOCHE FROG VESSEL
Moche potters based their designs on both fanciful and realistic images. They modeled many animals, human figures, and plants. Vessels with stirrup spouts often served as libation vessels—containers for making liquid offerings to the gods.

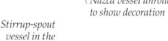

Nazca vessel unrolled to show decoration

NAZCA POT
The Nazca civilization was distinctive for its pottery, decorated in many colors with both realistic and mythological creatures, such as this being with a human body.

Stirrup-spout vessel in the shape of a frog

Jade and shell eyes *Pieces of shell*

CHICKEN VESSEL
This is a good example of the creativity and imagination of the potters from Teotihuacan. How a pot was made, its shape, and the motifs decorating it help researchers discover when it was made.

Conch shells adorn body

PAINTING PALETTE
The potters of Teotihuacan used both vegetable and mineral pigments, and it is likely that they used some kind of palette to mix their colors. This pottery object may have been used as a such a palette.

FIGURINE AND MOLD
Made using a mold, this small clay artifact depicts a female figure holding two children. It may represent a midwife or a goddess of fertility and childbirth.

Clay goddess

Mold for goddess

Center of bowl is decorated with a glyph of a deer

CHOLULA BOWL
The city of Cholula was sacred to the Aztecs, and its pottery was highly prized. One style of decoration used only two colors, as seen on this bowl.

Hummingbird perched on rim

This urn contained human ashes

MIXTEC CUP
This beautiful Mixtec cup is decorated with a hummingbird perched on the rim. The base has the characteristic step-fret motif often used by Mixtec artists.

Urn found at the Great Temple of the Aztecs

Step-fret motif

FUNERARY URN
Some pottery vessels were not painted, but instead the decoration was cut into the surface. The picture on one side of this urn is of a bearded god wearing a necklace. He holds a spear thrower in one hand, and spears in the other.

47

Featherwork

THE BRIGHT COLORS and natural sheen of tropical bird feathers made them a valuable item for trade and tribute in Mesoamerica and in the Andean region of South America. Tropical birds were hunted and raised in captivity for their feathers, which were worked into stunning patterns and designs. For the Mesoamericans, the iridescent green feathers of the quetzal were the most prized. The Incas used feathers as part of their dress and wove them into clothing for special occasions. They also used them to decorate headdresses and tunics, and to make mosaics (designs of feathers glued to a backing to decorate hard items such as shields). The skilled Aztec featherworkers made beautiful garments only for the nobility, while the Maya made superb headdresses that were extended at the back to make the wearer look like a bird that had just landed.

FEATHER MOSAICS
Ancient Mexico had a guild of expert featherworkers who used intricate methods of gluing and weaving feather mosaics. These methods were studied and illustrated by a Spanish friar (priest) called Bernardino de Sahagún.

FEATHER SHIRT AND HEADDRESS
This type of feather shirt is known as a poncho. Each of the feathers has been carefully stitched to a cotton cloth to make up the design of stylized owls and fish. Several Peruvian cultures, including the Chimu and the Inca, had expert featherworkers.

Tall feather headdress

Fan made of macaw feathers

Holder formed from braided brown wool

WAVE OF COLOR
The ancient Peruvians made very colorful fans using feathers from tropical birds. These fans were useful for keeping cool in hot climates. The Peruvians made many practical objects with feathers—especially the feathers of parrots and macaws, which were their favorite birds.

FEATHER HEADDRESS
This simple Peruvian headdress was possibly made from feathers taken from birds in the Amazon region. Items made from the feathers of exotic birds were status symbols.

Strings were used to tie the headdress around the head

MOCTEZUMA'S HEADDRESS?
This is a replica of a headdress said to have belonged to Moctezuma II, the last Aztec ruler. The headdress may have been part of the booty sent by Cortés to Spain (pp. 62–63). It is has green quetzal feathers, blue cotinga feathers, and gold disks.

Headdress contains the feathers of at least 250 birds

Fan has a butterfly on this side and a flower on the other

Feather headdress

MEXICAN FAN
This fan was made with the feathers of several species of bird. Sumptuous fans like this were used by dignitaries.

Bamboo handle

Cloak of yellow and green feathers

Rear view

Front view

Side view

WARRIOR OUTFIT
An Aztec warrior's rank was reflected in the type of feather suit he wore. This elaborate suit, complete with shield and headdress, was worn by a high-ranking warrior.

Feather headdress

Feather suit belonging to a warrior of high status

Feather shield

FEATHERS IN STONE
This carved stone Atlantean figure from a temple at Chichen Itza is dressed in a full-length feather cloak and a feather headdress. It was once painted all over, and the two watercolors show how it would probably have looked.

REBUILDING THE PAST
Watercolors like the one above by the British artist Adela Breton give us an idea of how sculptures were painted in pre-Hispanic times, and of the original appearance of the buildings at Chichen Itza.

Feather suit

Precious metals

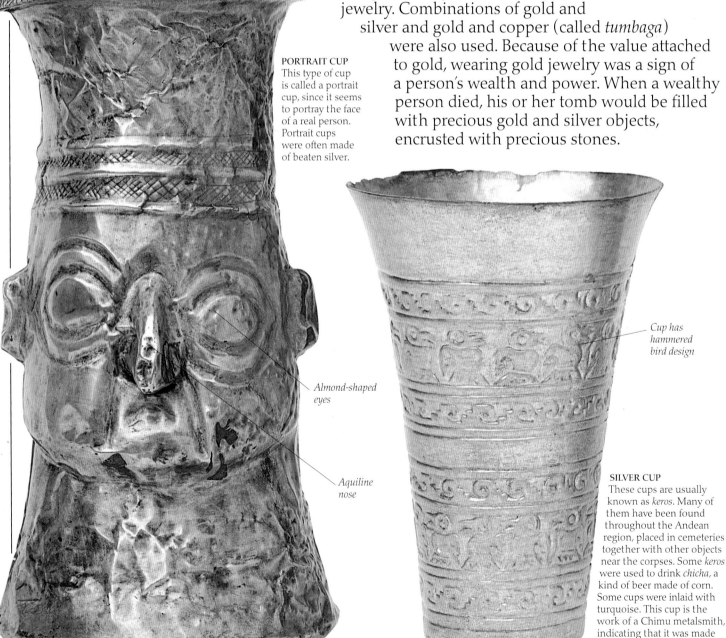

LIP ORNAMENT
Eagle heads like
this one made
by the Mixtecs
were popular as decoration for lip
plugs, or labrets. The Mixtecs produced
most of the gold work for the Aztec
elite. Labrets were inserted through
a hole made below the bottom lip.

THE PERUVIAN TRADITION of crafting
magnificent artifacts from precious metals
began 3,500 years ago, the age of the oldest
piece of precious metalwork found in the
Andes. Methods of metalworking gradually
developed, and metals were widely worked in
South America before the Christian era. They
were introduced to Mesoamerica in about
850 BCE. Some of the most common precious
metals in the Americas are gold, silver, and
platinum. These were mostly used for
making ritual objects, trinkets, and
jewelry. Combinations of gold and
silver and gold and copper (called *tumbaga*)
were also used. Because of the value attached
to gold, wearing gold jewelry was a sign of
a person's wealth and power. When a wealthy
person died, his or her tomb would be filled
with precious gold and silver objects,
encrusted with precious stones.

GOLD CREATURE
The ancient South
American goldsmiths
produced many fantastic
creatures. This figure is
a mixture of human
and animal forms.

PORTRAIT CUP
This type of cup
is called a portrait
cup, since it seems
to portray the face
of a real person.
Portrait cups
were often made
of beaten silver.

*Almond-shaped
eyes*

*Aquiline
nose*

*Cup has
hammered
bird design*

SILVER CUP
These cups are usually
known as *keros*. Many of
them have been found
throughout the Andean
region, placed in cemeteries
together with other objects
near the corpses. Some *keros*
were used to drink *chicha*, a
kind of beer made of corn.
Some cups were inlaid with
turquoise. This cup is the
work of a Chimu metalsmith,
indicating that it was made
before the Incan period.

50

ELEGANT NECKLACE
Of the few gold objects that have survived from the Basin of Mexico, most have been found at the Great Temple of the Aztecs. The beads of this necklace were made of hollow gold. Some of them are plain, while others are decorated with a spiral design.

Thunderbolt

BAT RATTLE
This cast-gold rattle represents a bat god. The god is holding a thunderbolt in one hand and a throwing stick in the other.

GOLD IN THE NOSE
This Mixtec ornament is one of the few surviving nose plugs. Some nose ornaments are in the shape of butterflies and other creatures. The beauty of this one lies in its simplicity.

PANNING FOR GOLD
Most of the gold used by the Peruvian Indians was obtained from "placer" mines in rivers, where the gold is near the surface. They used fire-hardened digging sticks to break up the soil and shallow trays in which to carry and wash it.

Charcoal-heated furnace, kept hot by blowing through a tube

Figure holds a standard or banner

Hooked earrings

LIME SCOOPS
These tiny lime scoops were used in the preparation of a drug called *coca*. Powdered lime was scooped onto a *coca* leaf, made into a ball, and chewed.

Handle has figure of a hummingbird

GOLDSMITH
The goldsmith had a high status in Aztec society. He made the most intricate objects using the "lost wax" method. First he made an intricately carved beeswax mold and covered it with a layer of clay. When the mold was heated, the melted wax flowed out, and the mold was filled with molten metal. In this illustration, the goldsmith is about to pour molten gold into a mold.

Handle has figure of a monkey

Stylized Incan llama figure, made of gold

MIXTEC GOLD FIGURE
This figure is probably the work of a Mixtec goldsmith. It shows man holding a shield and darts, with a pendant around his neck from which three bells hang. He is well attired, indicating that he is a member of the elite, a ruler, or an important warrior, and he is clad with gold—in other words, with wealth and power.

GOLD LLAMA
The Incas made vessels and figures using the casting method, by pouring molten metal into a mold. Items like this llama figure were sometimes partly soldered together, too.

Precious stones

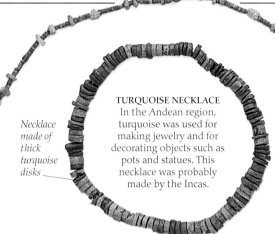

TURQUOISE NECKLACE
In the Andean region, turquoise was used for making jewelry and for decorating objects such as pots and statues. This necklace was probably made by the Incas.

Necklace made of thick turquoise disks

Red shell beads

THE INCAS, MAYA, AND AZTECS had a taste for all kinds of stones, and their skilled craftsmen fashioned exquisite objects from them. The Mesoamerican people favored stones of different colors with shiny surfaces, including jade and green stones in general, turquoise, onyx, rock crystal, and porphyry (a dark red rock). They used them to make jewelry and a variety of containers, sculptures, and masks. Jade was the most precious material to the Mesoamerican people. It was associated with water, the life-giving fluid, and with the color of the corn plant, their staple food. Turquoise was also highly valued and was laboriously worked both in Mesoamerica and in the Andean regions. The Incas used it as inlay in gold and silver objects.

TURQUOISE AND GOLD NECKLACE
Turquoise was highly valued in the Andean region. Only a few artifacts, like this delicate Incan necklace, have survived.

CHIMU WOMAN
This Chimu figurine (left) is of a woman wearing a headdress and a necklace strung with various beads, perhaps shells and stones.

Pieces of turquoise

Hollow gold bead

LIKE FATHER, LIKE SON
Craftsmen, such as this precious-stone cutter (called a lapidary), passed their skills on to their sons, who would take up their trade upon reaching manhood. The Aztecs believed that the arts of the lapidary and the goldsmith came from the Toltecs, who had received their skills from the god Quetzalcoatl.

Detail from Codex Mendoza

VAMPIRE BAT
This Zapotec mosaic mask is made of 25 pieces of jade. It is in the shape of a human head covered by a bat mask. The bat was an important symbol in the art of the Zapotec people.

Eyes made of shell

ONYX CUP
In Mesoamerica, onyx was used for making objects for the elite. The craftsman would begin with a large lump of onyx, cutting out the center with obsidian tools (above). Many onyx objects are rounded, like the cup shown below, as this was the easiest shape to produce.

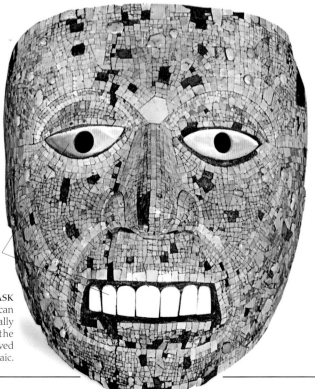

Eyes and teeth made of shell

TURQUOISE MASK
One of the most remarkable Mesoamerican arts was that of mosaic making, especially using turquoise. This mask, representing the god Quetzalcoatl, is one of the best preserved examples of Mexican turquoise mosaic.

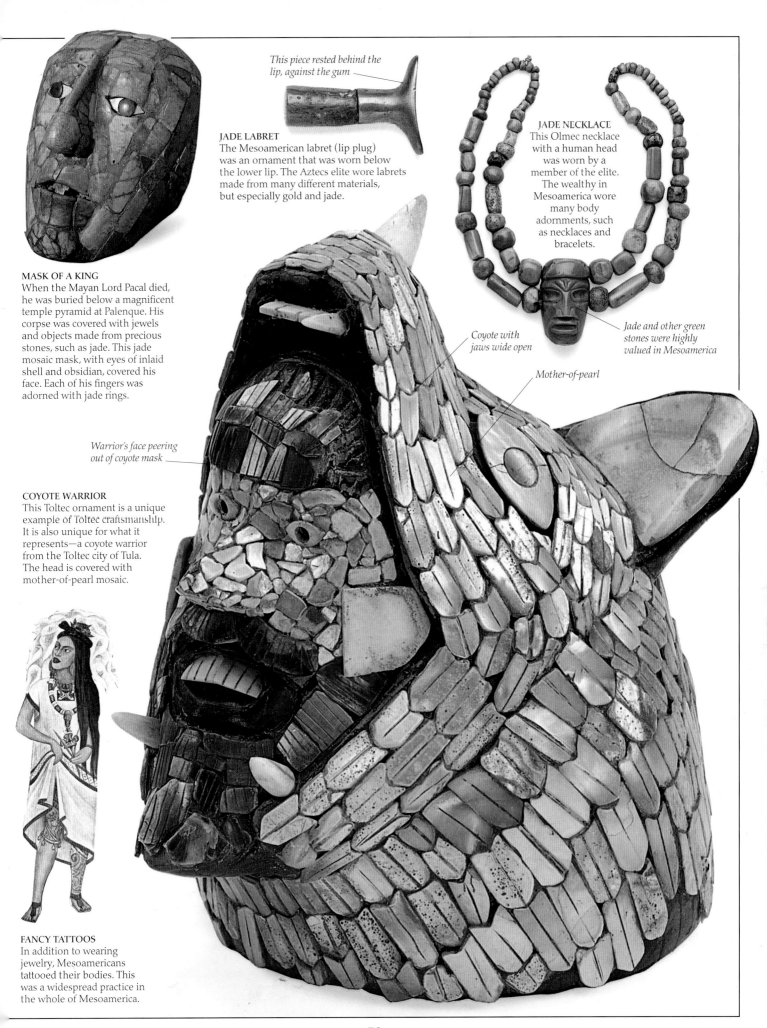

MASK OF A KING
When the Mayan Lord Pacal died, he was buried below a magnificent temple pyramid at Palenque. His corpse was covered with jewels and objects made from precious stones, such as jade. This jade mosaic mask, with eyes of inlaid shell and obsidian, covered his face. Each of his fingers was adorned with jade rings.

Warrior's face peering out of coyote mask

COYOTE WARRIOR
This Toltec ornament is a unique example of Toltec craftsmanship. It is also unique for what it represents—a coyote warrior from the Toltec city of Tula. The head is covered with mother-of-pearl mosaic.

FANCY TATTOOS
In addition to wearing jewelry, Mesoamericans tattooed their bodies. This was a widespread practice in the whole of Mesoamerica.

This piece rested behind the lip, against the gum

JADE LABRET
The Mesoamerican labret (lip plug) was an ornament that was worn below the lower lip. The Aztecs elite wore labrets made from many different materials, but especially gold and jade.

JADE NECKLACE
This Olmec necklace with a human head was worn by a member of the elite. The wealthy in Mesoamerica wore many body adornments, such as necklaces and bracelets.

Jade and other green stones were highly valued in Mesoamerica

Coyote with jaws wide open

Mother-of-pearl

Masks

For hundreds of years, masks fashioned from materials such as gold, obsidian, jade, and wood—some inlaid with turquoise and coral—have been worn in the Americas. Masks were commonly placed over mummy bundles to protect the deceased from the dangers of the afterlife. They were also worn during festivals. Among the Incas and the Aztecs, for whom music and dance (pp. 56–57) were a form of religious expression, masks and costumes had a symbolic meaning. Even today, people in Mesoamerica and in the Andean region still wear masks for festivals.

HUMAN MASK
Found at the Great Temple of the Aztecs, this finely carved greenstone mask was an offering to the gods. It is inlaid with shell and obsidian, and its ear lobes are pierced so that ear plugs can be attached.

Jade ear plug

Holes in mask may have had hair threaded through them

BEATEN COPPER MASK
Masks such as this copper one (left) have been found on mummies in many Andean burial sites. The wealthier the individual, the more elaborate was their burial—and the more expensive the fabrics that wrapped and decorated the mummy bundle.

Mask made of stone

FACE VALUE
Many objects from the Mezcala region, including masks, were found at the Great Temple of the Aztecs. This mask was paid as tribute to the Aztecs (pp. 26–27).

MAYAN HEAD
Many heads and masks give an idea of what people looked like. This head shows that the Maya practiced cranial deformation, which means that they forced the top of the head to grow taller and slope backward.

JEWELED MASK
This Chimu funerary mask is made of thin sheet-gold. It would have been placed over a mummy's face. The nose ornament, decorated with gold disks, was made separately.

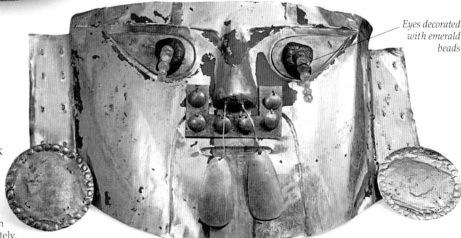

Eyes decorated with emerald beads

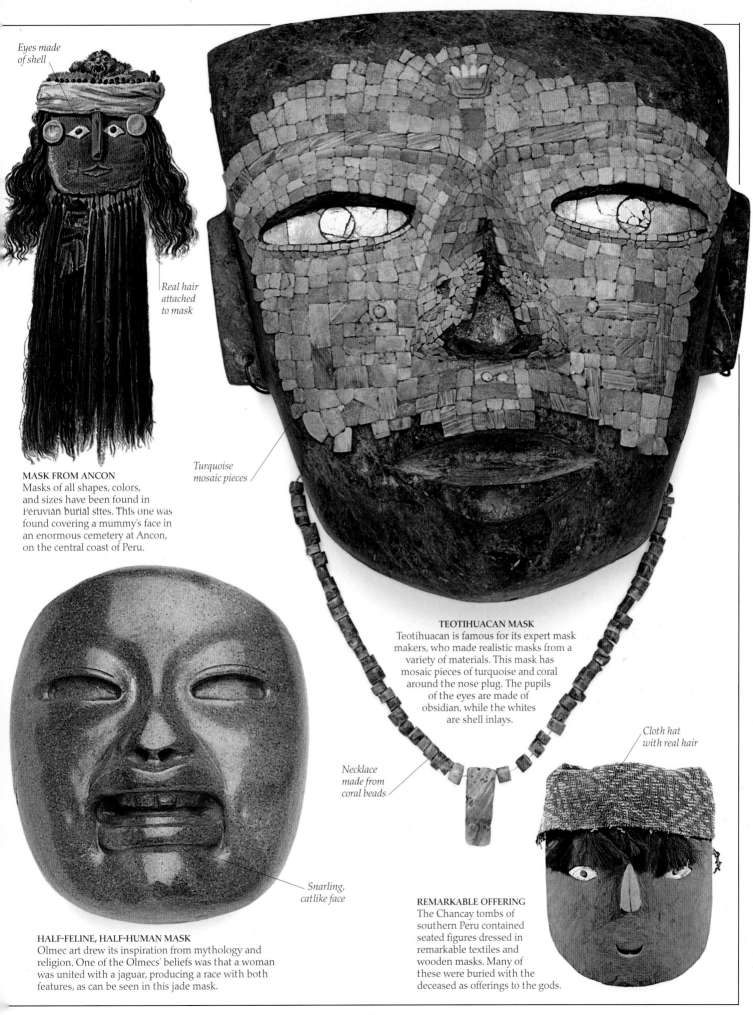

MASK FROM ANCON
Masks of all shapes, colors, and sizes have been found in Peruvian burial sites. This one was found covering a mummy's face in an enormous cemetery at Ancon, on the central coast of Peru.

Eyes made of shell

Real hair attached to mask

Turquoise mosaic pieces

TEOTIHUACAN MASK
Teotihuacan is famous for its expert mask makers, who made realistic masks from a variety of materials. This mask has mosaic pieces of turquoise and coral around the nose plug. The pupils of the eyes are made of obsidian, while the whites are shell inlays.

Necklace made from coral beads

Cloth hat with real hair

HALF-FELINE, HALF-HUMAN MASK
Olmec art drew its inspiration from mythology and religion. One of the Olmecs' beliefs was that a woman was united with a jaguar, producing a race with both features, as can be seen in this jade mask.

Snarling, catlike face

REMARKABLE OFFERING
The Chancay tombs of southern Peru contained seated figures dressed in remarkable textiles and wooden masks. Many of these were buried with the deceased as offerings to the gods.

Music and dance

MOCHE FLAUTIST
Many Moche vases are realistic portraits of people and their pastimes. This one shows that flutes were played in the Andean region.

MUSIC, SONG, AND DANCE were an important part of Mesoamerican and South American life. Scenes of people playing music and dancing decorate many pottery vases, especially those produced by the Moche potters. The most common instruments in both Mesoamerica and South America were rattles, whistles, trumpets, flutes, copper bells, and shells. String instruments were practically unknown in the Americas.

The music in South America was not very varied, and often musical instruments only played one tone. For these civilizations, music and dance were closely linked to religion. Everyone, from rulers to peasants, took part in dances that were performed especially for their gods.

End of rattle in the shape of a dog's head

CLAY TRUMPET
Moche trumpets came in straight and coiled shapes. The one shown here ends in two catlike heads, which may represent a god. This shape of coil is typical of Moche trumpets.

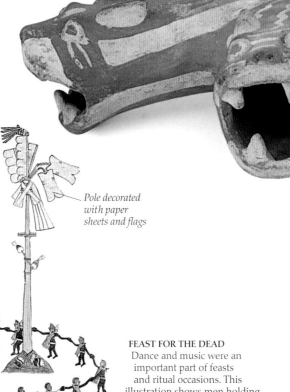

Catlike heads have gaping, snarling jaws with bared fangs

Pole decorated with paper sheets and flags

Carving shows a person with loose hair, wearing a tasseled headdress decorated with feathers

Aztec *teponaztli* (horizontal drum)

FEAST FOR THE DEAD
Dance and music were an important part of feasts and ritual occasions. This illustration shows men holding hands, dancing around a pole, at a feast for the dead. The pole is festooned with paper sheets and three big flags, one of which has a feather decoration. The Aztecs adorned an image of the dead person with flags. This feast lasted all day, and people danced to the beat of the drum, played by a priest. The dancers in this scene were captives who were later burned as sacrifice.

Drum covered with a cat's pelt

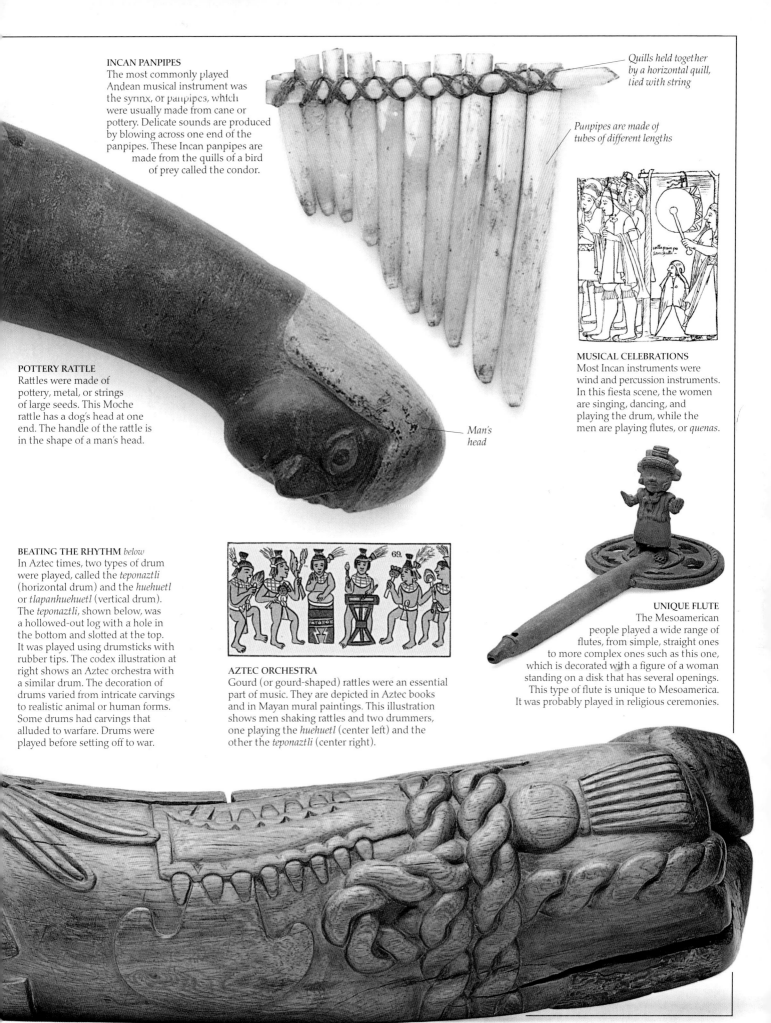

INCAN PANPIPES
The most commonly played Andean musical instrument was the syrinx, or panpipes, which were usually made from cane or pottery. Delicate sounds are produced by blowing across one end of the panpipes. These Incan panpipes are made from the quills of a bird of prey called the condor.

Quills held together by a horizontal quill, tied with string

Panpipes are made of tubes of different lengths

POTTERY RATTLE
Rattles were made of pottery, metal, or strings of large seeds. This Moche rattle has a dog's head at one end. The handle of the rattle is in the shape of a man's head.

Man's head

MUSICAL CELEBRATIONS
Most Incan instruments were wind and percussion instruments. In this fiesta scene, the women are singing, dancing, and playing the drum, while the men are playing flutes, or *quenas*.

BEATING THE RHYTHM *below*
In Aztec times, two types of drum were played, called the *teponaztli* (horizontal drum) and the *huehuetl* or *tlapanhuehuetl* (vertical drum). The *teponaztli*, shown below, was a hollowed-out log with a hole in the bottom and slotted at the top. It was played using drumsticks with rubber tips. The codex illustration at right shows an Aztec orchestra with a similar drum. The decoration of drums varied from intricate carvings to realistic animal or human forms. Some drums had carvings that alluded to warfare. Drums were played before setting off to war.

AZTEC ORCHESTRA
Gourd (or gourd-shaped) rattles were an essential part of music. They are depicted in Aztec books and in Mayan mural paintings. This illustration shows men shaking rattles and two drummers, one playing the *huehuetl* (center left) and the other the *teponaztli* (center right).

UNIQUE FLUTE
The Mesoamerican people played a wide range of flutes, from simple, straight ones to more complex ones such as this one, which is decorated with a figure of a woman standing on a disk that has several openings. This type of flute is unique to Mesoamerica. It was probably played in religious ceremonies.

Sports and games

EVERY ASPECT of Aztec life revolved around religion, including sports and games. The two main games played by the Aztecs were *patolli*, a board game similar to backgammon, and the ball game *ulama*, which was played in Mesoamerica long before the Aztecs by other ancient Mexican civilizations such as the Maya. In addition to being a sport, the ball game had a religious meaning. The ball court represented the world and the ball stood for the Moon and the Sun. Bets were placed on the outcome of the game, and some players lost everything they had— including their lives.

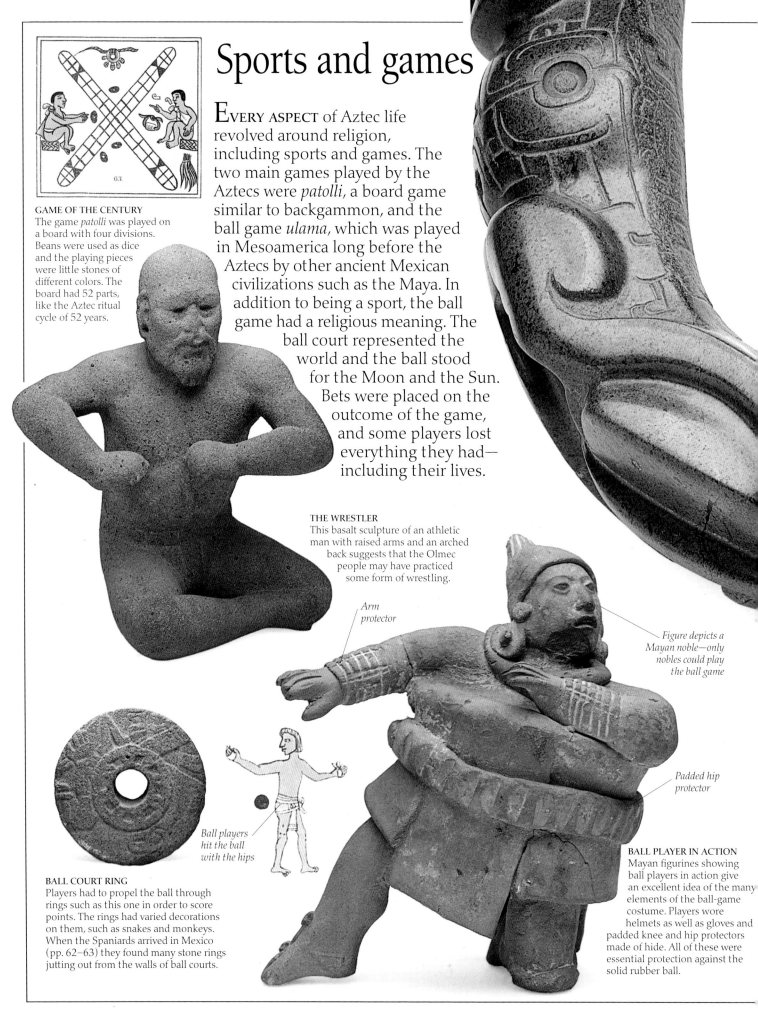

GAME OF THE CENTURY
The game *patolli* was played on a board with four divisions. Beans were used as dice and the playing pieces were little stones of different colors. The board had 52 parts, like the Aztec ritual cycle of 52 years.

THE WRESTLER
This basalt sculpture of an athletic man with raised arms and an arched back suggests that the Olmec people may have practiced some form of wrestling.

Arm protector

Figure depicts a Mayan noble—only nobles could play the ball game

Padded hip protector

Ball players hit the ball with the hips

BALL COURT RING
Players had to propel the ball through rings such as this one in order to score points. The rings had varied decorations on them, such as snakes and monkeys. When the Spaniards arrived in Mexico (pp. 62–63) they found many stone rings jutting out from the walls of ball courts.

BALL PLAYER IN ACTION
Mayan figurines showing ball players in action give an excellent idea of the many elements of the ball-game costume. Players wore helmets as well as gloves and padded knee and hip protectors made of hide. All of these were essential protection against the solid rubber ball.

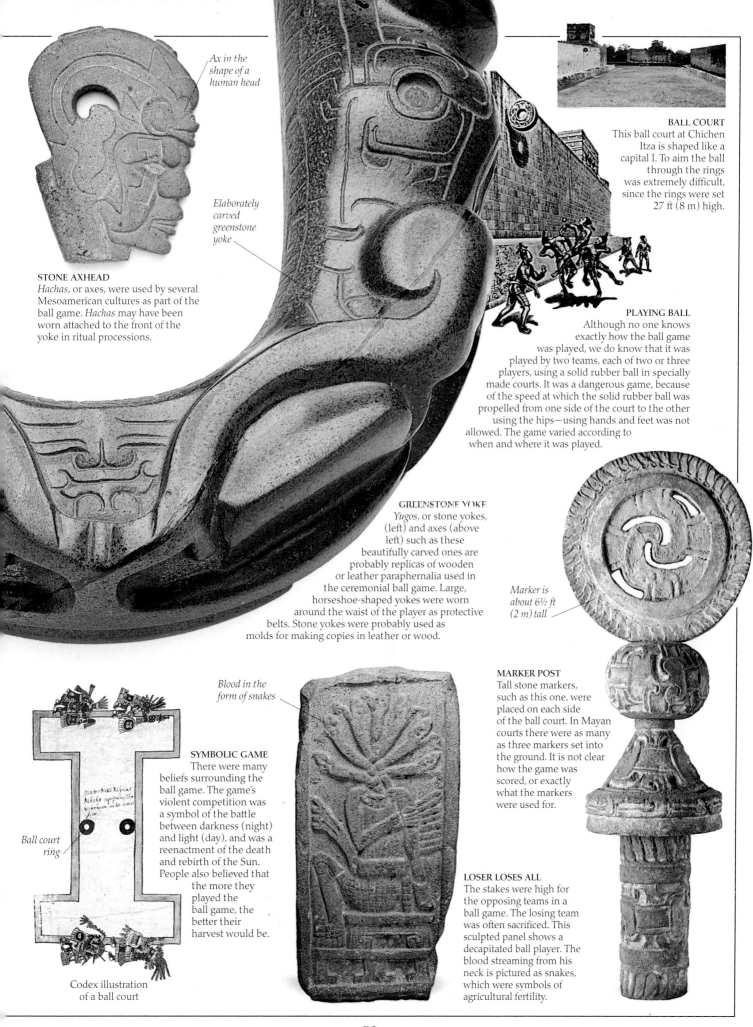

STONE AXHEAD

Hachas, or axes, were used by several Mesoamerican cultures as part of the ball game. *Hachas* may have been worn attached to the front of the yoke in ritual processions.

Ax in the shape of a human head

Elaborately carved greenstone yoke

BALL COURT

This ball court at Chichen Itza is shaped like a capital I. To aim the ball through the rings was extremely difficult, since the rings were set 27 ft (8 m) high.

PLAYING BALL

Although no one knows exactly how the ball game was played, we do know that it was played by two teams, each of two or three players, using a solid rubber ball in specially made courts. It was a dangerous game, because of the speed at which the solid rubber ball was propelled from one side of the court to the other using the hips—using hands and feet was not allowed. The game varied according to when and where it was played.

GREENSTONE YOKE

Yugos, or stone yokes, (left) and axes (above left) such as these beautifully carved ones are probably replicas of wooden or leather paraphernalia used in the ceremonial ball game. Large, horseshoe-shaped yokes were worn around the waist of the player as protective belts. Stone yokes were probably used as molds for making copies in leather or wood.

Marker is about 6½ ft (2 m) tall

SYMBOLIC GAME

There were many beliefs surrounding the ball game. The game's violent competition was a symbol of the battle between darkness (night) and light (day), and was a reenactment of the death and rebirth of the Sun. People also believed that the more they played the ball game, the better their harvest would be.

Blood in the form of snakes

Ball court ring

Codex illustration of a ball court

MARKER POST

Tall stone markers, such as this one, were placed on each side of the ball court. In Mayan courts there were as many as three markers set into the ground. It is not clear how the game was scored, or exactly what the markers were used for.

LOSER LOSES ALL

The stakes were high for the opposing teams in a ball game. The losing team was often sacrificed. This sculpted panel shows a decapitated ball player. The blood streaming from his neck is pictured as snakes, which were symbols of agricultural fertility.

Bestiary

ANIMAL LIFE IN MESOMERICA and South America was rich and varied. Animals played an important part in everyday life and also in religion. Many works of art included images of animals that were significant to the local people, such as foxes, owls, jaguars, llamas, hummingbirds, and eagles. Some animals were domesticated—for example, the turkey and the dog in Mesoamerica, and the llama and the alpaca in the Andean region. With their relatives, the guanacos and vicuñas, llamas and alpacas were valued for their wool and meat, and also as beasts of burden. Deer, rabbits, ducks, and many other kinds of edible bird abounded in both regions. The tropical forests were home to the jaguar, the largest cat in the world, which was worshiped and feared along with snakes.

BIRD ASSORTMENT
Mesoamerica had a variety of brilliantly colored tropical birds, including parrots, macaws, and quetzals. Their feathers were used to decorate a range of objects and clothes (pp. 48–49).

QUETZAL BIRD
This bird was greatly valued by the ancient Mesoamericans, for whom its long, deep-green feathers were as precious as jade or gold. Some of their gods were covered in quetzal feathers, and the bird's feathers were also used to make the headdresses of rulers and kings.

BIRD TAPESTRY
The Andean Paracas culture was renowned for its abundant, ornate textiles that were placed alongside the dead. This textile fragment is decorated with a typical Paracas design of stylized birds.

Figure has feline claws and ears and a stylized tail

FABRIC ANIMAL
Many textiles from Paracas are woven or embroidered with animal images, often in a stylized form. Sometimes it is difficult to identify the animal in question, because of the geometric forms.

FOX
Animals that hunted and killed other animals, such as the fox, were in turn hunted by the Aztecs and the Incas. This Moche vessel depicts the face of a snarling fox.

This an example of plumbate pottery—lead in the clay gives the pot a metallic finish

TOLTEC CERAMIC DOG
Some breeds of dog were fattened and eaten by the Aztecs and the Maya, but the Incas considered eating dog meat a disgusting habit. The Mesoamericans used dogs as companions in hunting expeditions. According to their religion, dogs were also necessary for the journey to the afterlife, since they helped the dead cross rivers.

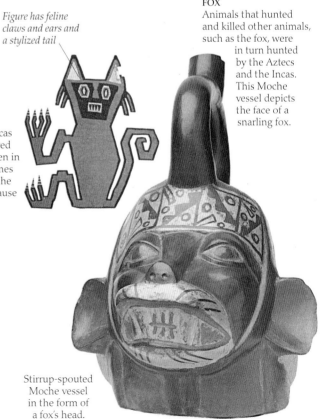

Stirrup-spouted Moche vessel in the form of a fox's head.

Vicuñas
on the
grasslands
of the
Andean
mountains

ARMADILLO
The Aztecs ate the
meat of the armadillo,
which is white and
tastes like chicken.
Among the Maya,
the armadillo was
associated with
the afterlife.

*Some armadillos
grow to a length
of 4 ft (120 cm)*

The armadillo is a nocturnal mammal
that lives in tropical areas

*Alpacas can reach a
height of 50 in (130 cm)
at the shoulder*

ALPACA
The alpaca lives in the Andean highlands. It was
kept in herds by the ancient Peruvians because,
along with the vicuña, its long wool was ideal for
weaving. Its relatives, the guanaco and the llama,
were killed for food, although the llama was mostly
used for carrying loads. The ancient Andean people
made offerings to the alpaca, because it
made an important contribution
to their livelihood.

VICUÑAS
Like the
alpaca, the
vicuña (above)
was a good
wool-producing
animal. Vicuñas
gave the most
elegant, silklike
wool. Garments
woven from
vicuña wool
were worn by
Incan nobility.

Zapotec jaguar vessel, probably
used as an incense burner

Ocelot

OCELOT
This wild cat is sometimes known
as the Mexican tiger. The ocelot
was a greatly feared creature.
Some warriors wore ocelot skins
when going
into battle.

Puma

PUMA
The puma is found in a wide range
of habitats in the Americas, including
mountains and tropical forests. It was hunted
for its skin by ancient American peoples.

Jaguar

SACRED JAGUAR
The jaguar was one of the
most powerful symbols in
Mesoamerica and South
America. Its strength,
ferocity, cunning, and
hunting ability were
greatly admired. The
Zapotec vessel (far right)
is in the shape of a jaguar
standing on three legs.

*Leg decorated with
head of baby jaguar*

The Spanish conquest

When the Spanish arrived in the Americas, they knew nothing about the Mesoamerican and Andean cultures with their powerful empires, elaborate palaces, and religions that reached into every part of their lives. Neither did the inhabitants of the Americas have any knowledge of the Spanish. Many omens had forewarned Moctezuma II, the Aztec ruler, of an imminent disaster. The Incan ruler Huayna Capac, too, had heard that strange, bearded men had appeared on the coast. Hernándo Cortés entered Mexico in 1519 and Francisco Pizarro arrived in Peru in 1532. Although having few soldiers, the Spanish armies, with their horses and cannons, were stronger. Many local people joined forces with the Spaniards, angry at having to pay heavy tributes. Within a short time, the world of the Aztecs and the Incas was destroyed, their temples razed to the ground, and their emperors murdered. The Maya resisted until 1542, when the Spanish established a capital at Mérida.

MOCTEZUMA GREETS CORTÉS
When they first met, Cortés greeted Moctezuma with a bow, and Moctezuma handed him splendid presents of gold, precious stones such as jade, and feather objects. Cortés was on horseback and Moctezuma was carried in a litter. The Spanish soldiers were dressed in steel armor, while the Aztecs wore simple cotton cloaks. This meeting would prove decisive in the conquest of Mexico. Moctezuma at this point was in two minds about the true nature of Cortés— was he human or god, their enemy or their savior? The events that followed proved Cortés to be the former.

MASSACRE
The Spanish *conquistadores* went in search of riches. If they met any resistance from the native people, the *conquistadores* killed them. This illustration depicts an expedition to Michoacan in the west of Mexico, where many local noblemen were killed for refusing to say where their treasures were hidden.

Warriors from the state of Tlaxcala supported the conquistadores

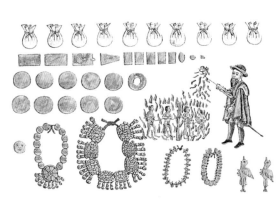

GOLDEN DEATH
This scene from the Codex Kingsborough shows a Spanish tribute collector punishing the Mexican Indians at Tepetlaoztoc. A Spanish tribute collector was a privileged colonialist known as an *encomendero*. The Indians being burned were late in paying their tribute. The tribute demanded consisted of bundles of corn and gold jewelry.

Doubloon coins made from gold mined in South America

A DISEASE THAT ONLY GOLD COULD CURE

To coerce the people of Mesoamerica and South America to give them their gold, the Spanish often told them that they suffered from a disease that only gold could cure. Cortés and Pizarro both went to the Americas in search of gold, and they found a great deal of it. At the start of the conquest, Cortés sent booty to King Charles V of Spain consisting of gold and silver objects and many other goods. Over the years, huge quantities of gold were shipped to Spain. Today, the ceilings of many Spanish churches are gilded with gold from the Americas.

PUNISHMENT

This illustration shows some of the punishments inflicted by the Spanish on the Incan people. They included beating them and hanging them upside down. The cruelty of many of the *conquistadores* made some Spanish friars devote their lives to denouncing the behavior of their compatriots.

Francisco Pizarro, the conqueror of Peru

GREED FOR GOLD

This caricature shows a greedy Francisco Pizarro contemplating gold from his new Peruvian mine. Pizarro did not understand the civilization that he helped to destroy.

Wooden Inca *kero*, or cup

CONQUEROR'S CUP

This wooden *kero* cup portrays the conqueror of Peru, Francisco Pizarro. Under Pizarro, Spanish control was established over the Incan Empire. The Spanish forced people to abandon their irrigated lands and demanded that they mine more precious metals. Christianity was imposed upon the Incas, but they were slow to accept the new religion and continued in their old practices. The Incas continued with some of their crafts, such as weaving and making wooden *keros* like this one, which may have been made for Pizarro himself.

Did you know?

AMAGING FACTS

The Maya and the Aztecs were excellent beekeepers. They raised stingless bees for honey, which was harvested once a year for medicine and for sweetening food.

Chewing gum may have been an Aztec innovation. The chicozapote tree, one of the most common in Mesoamerica, produces a resin known as chicle, from which chewing gum is made. The Aztecs chewed on chicle to clean their teeth.

Chicozapote tree

The Mayan people had a zodiac of constellations made up of animals. These included the turtle, the bat, the jaguar, and the turkey. The only animal common to both Mayan and Western zodiac signs is the scorpion.

The Aztecs used a beverage made from live toads steeped in sugar in some of their religious rituals. Toads of the *Bufo* genus secrete toxins from their parotid glands which, when consumed, produce hallucinations. Many Aztec medicines were based on these secretions.

Some Mayan temples featured a complex mosaic of stonework around the entrance door that gave the impression of the jaws of a monster, including stone snouts and fangs. This is because in Mayan belief the entrance to the underworld was thought of as the mouth of a monster. By entering a temple decorated in this way, priests believed they were literally stepping into the supernatural world.

Many Incan kings kept everything they had contact with, so that they could be buried with it. Tombs have been found containing hampers of used clothing, the king's dishes and cutlery, hair and nail clippings—even corncobs and old bones once gnawed on by the king.

In Mesoamerica, the jaguar (the largest cat of the Americas) was a symbol of royal power. Kings wore the pelt of a jaguar as part of their regalia, and jaguars were offered to the gods in sacrifice.

The Maya believed that slightly crossed eyes were beautiful. They dangled objects in front of their eyes in an attempt to cross them. Foreheads that sloped back were also considered beautiful. To achieve this, the Maya tied boards to babies' foreheads to mold their skulls into the desired shape. This process did not seem to harm the brain.

The Aztec Calendar Stone, carved in the early 16th century, is immense. It measures around 13 ft (4 m) in diameter and weighs 27 tons (24 metric tons). The Aztec solar year contained 18 months of 20 days each, with 5 extra days. Aztec priests used the calendar to keep track of important festival dates. The face of the stone contains various mythological and astrological figures and signs. The most important figure in the stone is Tonatiuh, the Sun god, located in the center.

Mayan artists, unlike those of many ancient cultures, often included their names on stone carvings and other works. There are also Mayan ceramics "signed" with the artist's name.

The large number and wide variety of musical instruments found in archeological sites in Mesoamerica indicate the important place of music and dance in cultural life. There were drums made of wood or clay topped with monkey skins; rattles made of turtle shells; hollow shakers filled with shells, seeds, or dried llama toenails; conch-shell trumpets; and flutes made from animal or human bones.

Clothing was an important status symbol among the Incas. The king had certain fabrics reserved for his use alone. His shirts were of the finest, most delicate cloth, embroidered with gold and silver and decorated with bird feathers. Some royal clothing was made of such difficult-to-produce fibers as bat hair.

Flute

Figures from mythology are shown on the calendar stone

Modern reconstruction of Aztec calendar

Mayan temple entrance resembling jaws

QUESTIONS AND ANSWERS

Q Why was the ball game, or *ulama* as it was known, so important?

A The Mesoamerican peoples were obsessed with *ulama*, not only as a sport played for general recreation, but also as a religious ritual. The ball game took place between competing teams of players, and may have symbolized the battles between the sky gods and the lords of the underworld, with the ball itself representing the Sun. In some games, the leader of a losing team was decapitated; his skull then formed the core of a new ball. In other games, the winning team's prize was to behead the unfortunate losers.

Disk inlaid in Mayan ball-court

Q What was in the water at the Sacred Cenote at Chichen Itza?

A Cenotes (natural wells formed after the roof of an underground river collapses) were important to the Maya. They considered them to be a way of communicating directly with Chac, the rain god, to ask for plentiful rain for the crops. For hundreds of years, people told tales of fabulous gold and jade objects tossed into these wells to appease Chac. An American consul to the region named Edward Thompson used his diplomatic skills to purchase the lands containing the Sacred Cenote at Chichen Itza, Mexico. Between 1904 and 1907, he hired men to dive into the murky waters and used a simple dredge to pull up hundreds of precious objects (and child-sized human bones). Many of them were removed from the country and displayed in the Peabody Museum in Boston. The Mexican authorities fought for decades for the return of the treasures, and they are now on display in the Regional Museum of Merida, Mexico.

Q Where was the City of the Gods, and why was it sacred to the Aztecs?

A The ruins of Teotihuacan lie just north of present-day Mexico City. Founded around 100 BCE, Teotihuacan grew to become the largest city in the Americas, with a population of about 150,000 people. Two huge step-pyramids, the Pyramid of the Sun and the Pyramid of the Moon, dominated its center. The Teotihuacan culture declined and the city was abandoned around 750 CE. The Aztecs made the city a pilgrimage site, since they believed that it was where the gods had gathered to create the Sun and the Moon.

View of Teotihuacan ruins along the Avenue of the Dead

Q Who rediscovered Machu Picchu, the lost city of the Incas?

A This incredible city was probably constructed by the Incas in the mid to late 15th century, and was inhabited until the Spanish conquest of Peru. Its large palace and temples surrounding a courtyard were not meant to be a "working" city, but a country retreat for the Incan nobility. The American archeologist Hiram Bingham, in the area to explore old Incan roads, encountered the city in 1911. He wrote a number of books and articles that introduced Machu Picchu to the rest of the world.

Q What is the mystery behind the Nazca lines in Peru?

A The Nazca people created hundreds of pictures in the Peruvian desert of birds, insects, mammals, fish, and plants. These immense "drawings" were made by arranging small stones on the desert flats. They may have been sacred pathways, since some of the lines meet at small shrines where offerings were made.

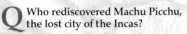

Nazca bird figure in the deserts of Peru

Q What happened to the Mesoamerican and Andean peoples after the Spanish conquest?

A Many people were captured and killed by the Spanish *conquistadores*; scores of others died from contact with new European diseases. The Spanish also enslaved people, sending them to mine precious metals. It is important to note that the people did not simply disappear. While Aztec, Inca, and Maya are generally used as historical terms, millions of their descendants still live in the region today and speak related languages.

Record breakers

OLDEST INTACT MAYAN MURAL
In 2002, archeologist William Saturno uncovered a near-pristine Mayan mural dating from 100 CE, in San Bartolo, Guatemala.

LARGEST BALL COURT IN MESOAMERICA
The court at Chichen Itza measures 551 ft (168 m) long and 229 ft (70 m) wide. Its acoustics are so good that you can stand at one end and hear people talking at the other.

TALLEST MAYAN PYRAMID
Erected around 741 CE, Temple IV at Tikal, Guatemala, rises to a height of 230 ft (70 m).

LARGEST ADOBE STRUCTURE IN SOUTH AMERICA
The base of the Temple of the Sun, near Trujillo, Peru, measures 730 ft (223 m) on each side. Built by the Moche, it was originally 200 ft (70 m) high.

LARGEST PREHISTORIC REPRESENTATION OF A HUMAN FIGURE IN THE WORLD
The geoglyph of the Giant of Atacama, located in Iquique, Chile, is 282 ft (86 m) long.

Timeline

THE SPANISH EXPLORERS who reached the Americas in the 16th century called it the New World, but there was nothing new about it to the civilizations they found there. The cultures of the Aztecs and the Maya of Mesoamerica and the Incas of South America had been thriving for centuries, and numerous other civilizations had risen and fallen during the preceding millennia. The people of these civilizations built spectacular cities, created masterpieces of art, established trading links, created religious traditions, and built vast political empires. This timeline will guide you through the cultural history of Mesoamerica and South America.

Moche owl figure

c. 13,000 BCE
Asian hunter-gatherers probably make the first crossings into Alaska and the Yukon in North America over the Bering Strait; by c. 11,000 BCE, there are people in Chile.

c. 7000 BCE
The first crops are grown in Mexico. Corn is first cultivated there in about 5,000 BCE.

c. 3500 BCE
The llama is first used as a pack animal in Peru; it is also used as a food source.

c. 3500 BCE
Cotton is grown as a crop in Peruvian villages. Women weave cloth from the cotton; they are often buried with their weaving baskets.

Cotton

2000 BCE–250 CE
The Preclassic Period of Mesoamerican history; the Olmecs dominate.

c. 1200 BCE
The rise of the Olmecs on the coast of the Gulf of Mexico. The Olmecs (believed to be the first civilization in North and Central America) thrive for 600 years. They are skilled sculptors and architects, as well as fishermen, farmers, and traders.

c. 1000 BCE
The Mayan culture of Mesoamerica is well established by now.

c. 600 BCE
The Oaxaca culture begins to overtake the Olmec culture. The Zapotec civilization is established with its capital in Monte Alban.

c. 500 BCE
The Paracas culture flourishes in Peru. The people are skilled at embroidery, using more than 100 colors in their elaborate works.

c. 200 BCE
The Nazca culture begins in southern Peru; its people are known for painted pottery as well as for creating large and mysterious geoglyphs in the desert.

c. 100 CE
The Moche civilization on the Peruvian coast begins. The Moche are excellent potters and the first South Americans to produce clay objects from molds. The people are also highly skilled weavers and goldsmiths.

250–900
The Classic Period of Mesoamerican history; the Maya dominate.

c. 250
The Mayan civilization of Guatemala, Honduras, and eastern Mexico enters the period of its greatest development. The Maya do not have a capital city or single ruler. Instead, each city governs itself.

c. 600
The Tiahuanaco Empire grows near Lake Titicaca in Bolivia, South America. Its people establish a leading trading center, the vast city of Tiahuanaco, which becomes home to more than 100,000 people. Their Peruvian neighbors, the Huari, share their religion and art styles, and together the two cultures control the entire Andean region.

c. 650
The Pyramid of the Sun is the center of civilization for the mighty Teotihuacan culture in Mexico. It is part of a large complex, linked by wide, straight streets, that comprises several vast pyramids, palaces, and other buildings of unknown use.

Pyramid of the Sun, Teotihuacan

c. 850

The Mayan civilization in the southern part of Mexico begins to fade. Over the next 200 years, Mayan control of northern Mexico also wanes. Battling empires emerge to take control of the region.

900–1519

The Postclassic Period of history in Mesoamerica.

c. 900–1000

The Toltecs build a capital at Tula, Mexico. Their culture blends aspects of Mayan culture with their own. They are excellent architects and artisans, and worship Quetzalcoatl (the Feathered Serpent) as a man-god. The Toltecs eventually settle in Chichen Itza and build amazing pyramids there.

c. 900

The kingdom of the Chancay flourishes on Peru's central coast. Its people develop a distinctive pottery style.

Chimu gold spoon

c. 1000

The Chimu culture is on the rise in Peru. Its people are skilled weavers, goldsmiths, and architects. They build their capital at Chan Chan, on the coast. The Chimu are eventually conquered by the Incas.

c. 1300

The Incas begin to expand their empire throughout the central Andes. They are ruled by Viracocha, the first major Incan empire builder.

c. 1325

The Aztecs found the city of Tenochtitlan (present-day Mexico City) on an island in Lake Texcoco.

c. 1400–1470

Both the Aztec and Incan empires expand rapidly. In 1426, the Aztecs make an alliance with neighboring cities to help concentrate power in Aztec emperor Itzcoatl's hands. They establish a vast trading empire and build spectacular temples and pyramids. By 1500, there are more than 10 million Aztec citizens. The Incan Empire is also growing. Around 1438, Viracocha dies; Pachacuti, his successor, expands the Incan Empire north to present-day Ecuador. The Incas develop a massive road network covering more than 19,000 miles (30,000 km). Relay runners stationed along the network carry urgent messages and military orders back and forth along the entire route.

1440–1468

Aztec emperor Moctezuma I and his army take control of large areas of eastern Mexico.

c. 1450

The Incan city of Machu Picchu is built on a remote mountain ridge above the Urubamba River in Peru.

1455

A huge temple is built to the Aztec war god *Huizilopochtli* in Tenochtitlan.

1470

The collapse of the Chimu culture in northern Peru.

1486–1502

The rule of the Aztec emperor Ahuitzotl. The Aztec Empire is at the height of its power in Mexico under Ahuitzotl's reign.

1513

Spanish explorer Vasco de Balboa crosses the Central American mainland and becomes the first European to see the Pacific Ocean.

Guaman Poma used drawings in his book, such as this one of a patient visiting a healer, because he felt that pictures were as persuasive as words

Moctezuma I in his royal attire

Cortés

1519

Spanish explorer and soldier Hernándo Cortés and a band of 500 men reach the Aztec capital of Tenochtitlan. The Aztec emperor Moctezuma II greets him as an honored guest, but Cortés betrays him, arresting him and killing hundreds of Aztec nobles. The remaining Aztecs revolt the following year, but Cortés eventually prevails, and the Aztec Empire falls.

1532–1533

With fewer than 200 armed soldiers fighting alongside him, the Spanish warrior Francisco Pizarro attacks the Incan emperor Atahualpa as he marches with his entourage to his coronation. Everyone is killed except for Atahualpa; his life is spared on the condition that he pay a ransom in silver and gold. Atahualpa hands over the treasure and is promptly strangled.

1542

The Spanish establish a capital at Merida, and the Mayan resistance comes to an end.

1615

Felipe Guaman Poma de Ayala, a native Incan, completes his 1,200-page work, *The First New Chronicle and Good Government*, illustrated with 400 pen-and-ink drawings of Incan and colonial life. He addresses the work to King Philip III of Spain, hoping to seek reform of Spanish colonial governance in order to save the Andean peoples from the destructive forces of colonialism.

Page from Guaman Poma's book

Find out more

THE CULTURES OF THE Aztecs, Incas, and Maya may have disappeared, but the wealth of relics and ruins left behind reveal much about these ancient peoples and their times. If you are able to visit Central or South America, you can explore the sites of these once-thriving cities and follow in the footsteps of the people who lived there. But there are plenty of other ways to learn more about these cultures. The Internet offers virtual tours of places such as ancient temples and sacred cities. Many museums contain excellent collections from these areas.

ENJOY A TREAT TO EAT
If you are hungry to learn more about the cultures you have read about in this book, try a taste of traditional Central and South American cuisine. Many restaurants feature foods based on the same staples—corn, squash, and beans—that fed the Aztecs, Incas, and Maya. Try your hand at cooking a traditional dish, such as tacos.

THE INCA TRAIL
Many of the sites sacred to the ancient Americans are now popular tourist destinations. For example, you can trek along the Inca Trail in Peru to the sacred Incan city of Machu Picchu. The Spanish invaders at the time of the conquest and during centuries of colonial rule had no idea that the city was even there. Machu Picchu is now a World Heritage site and has thousands of visitors each day.

SOUNDS OF THE PAST
Music was an important part of ancient South American and Mesoamerican religious rituals. Today, folk musicians keep the sounds of the past alive, performing traditional music on modern replicas of instruments used by Aztec, Incan, and Mayan musicians. These musicians perform in traditional costume. Check the Internet to find out if a group will be performing at a cultural festival near you.

USEFUL WEBSITES

www.mesoweb.com
Explore the cultures of Mesoamerica

www.ancientmexico.com
The history of ancient Mexico, with an interactive map

www.ancientperu.com
An in-depth look at the Incan universe

www.pbs.org/opb/conquistadors
The story of Spain's crusading adventurers

www.ballgame.org
The Mesoamerican ball game brought vividly to life

Places to Visit

METROPOLITAN MUSEUM OF ART, NEW YORK, NY
The museum's collection from the ancient Americas spans a 3,500 year period. It includes the world's most comprehensive collection of American gold.

THE PHILADELPHIA MUSUM OF ART, PHILADELPHIA, PA
Pre-Columbian objects, including two large Aztec structures, comprise some of oldest objects in the museum's collection.

THE FIELD MUSEUM, CHICAGO, IL
The Ancient Americas exhibit takes visitors on a journey through 13,000 years of human achievement.

DENVER ART MUSEUM, DENVER, CO
The Pre-Columbian art collection represents nearly every major culture in Mesoamerica, with a particular emphasis on Mayan ceramics.

ST. LOUIS ART MUSEUM, ST. LOUIS, MO
The Pre-Columbian collection contains works of art from peoples of traditional Mesoamerican cultures, including the Maya, Mixtecs, Aztecs, and Incas.

MUSEO NACIONAL DE ANTROPOLOGÍA, MEXICO CITY, MEXICO
This museum contains possibly the world's greatest collection of objects related to the Maya. Its interactive kiosks tell the stories behind some 500 important objects on display.

AZTEC DANCERS
Traditional Aztec dance troupes wear vivid costumes lavished with gold and silver embroidery and elaborate feather headdresses. These dancers are performing at a Native American heritage festival in the United States. Check listings or the Internet to find out if any traditional dance troupes are making an international tour.

VISIT A MUSEUM
Many art and anthropology museums feature important works from the Aztec, Incan, and Mayan civilizations. A museum collection might include examples of textiles, pottery, metalwork, featherwork, basketry, and artifacts crafted from precious stones. Check with travel books or use the Internet to find the best permanent collections (some of which are listed in the box, top right). Also look out for travelling exhibitions from museums in Central and South America.

TRAVEL TO ANCIENT SITES
Exploring the lands of the Aztecs, Incas, or Maya can be an awe-inspiring experience. These tourists are climbing a pyramid in Mexico. Use the Internet to find sites open to visitors. Joining a group tour may give you access to more sites, as well as a valuable commentary from tour guides.

Glossary

ADOBE A traditional building material made from clay, straw, and water, formed into blocks and dried.

AGAVE A tropical American plant with tough, sword-shaped leaves and flowers in tall spikes. In Mesoamerica, the plant's fibers were woven into cloth; people also sucked the sap directly from the plant.

Agave plant

ALPACA A member of the llama family from the South American Andes Mountains. Alpaca hair fiber is prized for the soft, lightweight, yet extremely warm wool that can be woven from it.

ARMADILLO A burrowing, nocturnal mammal covered in strong, horny plates; eaten by Mesoamerican peoples.

ATOLE A mush or thin porridge made with corn, popular in Mesoamerica. The Incas ate a similar dish, called *capia*.

CACAO A tropical evergreen tree. Its dried and partially fermented beans are removed from their pods and processed to make chocolate, cocoa powder, and cocoa butter.

CALPULLI An Aztec neighborhood with shared rights and responsibilities among the households. The *calpulli* was the basic unit of Aztec society.

CHACMOOL A Mesoamerican sculpture of a reclining figure holding a bowl on its lap or stomach. The bowl is thought to be a receptacle for holding blood and human hearts after a sacrifice.

CHASQUIS In Moche society, a runner who carried messages from one place to another.

CHINAMPAS In Aztec agriculture, narrow strips of land built in swampy lakes, with canals running between them. Each *chinampa* was built with layers of plants cut from the lake and fertile soil from the lake bed.

CODEX An ancient type of book, made of bark paper from the fig tree, cloth, or animal skin folded like a concertina; the name comes from *caudex*, the Latin for "tree bark."

COMAL A large clay disk used for cooking *tortillas* over an open fire.

CONQUEST The acquisition of a territory and its people by force.

CONQUISTADOR One of the 16th-century Spanish explorers who conquered lands in the Americas.

COPAL A brittle, aromatic resin burned as an incense offering in ancient times; now used in varnishes.

DOUBLOON An old Spanish gold coin.

EMBROIDERY The act of embellishing a fabric or garment with a decorative pattern using hand-stitched needlework.

ENCOMENDERO A privileged Spanish colonist during the Spanish conquest of the Americas. The *encomenderos* became an early colonial aristocracy.

FRESCO From the Italian word for "fresh," the technique of painting on wet plaster so that the pigments are absorbed by the plaster, becoming part of the wall itself. A form of fresco that was employed by the artisans of Teotihuacan.

FUNERARY MASK A mask, typically made of metal, that was sometimes placed on the faces of Inca mummies before burial.

Mesoamerican glyph carved in stone

GLYPH A picture used to represent a word or a group of words.

GOURD Any of a group of inedible, vine-growing fruits with hard rinds.

GREENSTONE A dark green, metamorphic rock that owes its coloring to the presence of the mineral chlorite.

HIEROGLYPHIC WRITING A system of writing in which the characters consist of realistic or stylized pictures of actual objects, animals, or humans, rather than letters or words.

HUACAS In the Andean regions, a variety of shrines and objects and the natural forces associated with them.

Detail from Codex Cospi, an Aztec calendar, showing a god attacking an ocelot warrior

JAGUAR A large, spotted cat of tropical America, similar to the leopard.

KERO A drinking vessel, made of metal or wood, traditionally used in Andean feasts.

LABRET A plug inserted through a piercing below the bottom lip.

Jade labret from Mesoamerica

LOOM A machine used to weave yarn into a fabric.

MACUAHUITL One of the Aztecs' main weapons; a wooden club edged with sharp obsidian blades.

MAGUEY A type of agave plant.

MAIZE A tall, annual, cereal grass bearing kernels on large ears of corn; a staple food in Mexico, and Central and South America.

MESOAMERICA The region of Mexico and Central America historically inhabited by the Aztecs, Maya, and related cultures.

METLATL A grinding stone, usually made from volcanic stone such as basalt. *Metlatl* were commonly found in the Mesoamerican kitchen and are still used today.

MUMMY A body embalmed and dried and wrapped for burial.

MUMMY BUNDLE A Mesoamerican mummy wrapped in textiles or reed matting and tied with ropes.

Incan mummy bundle

OBSIDIAN A volcanic glass that may be clear, black, brown, or green. Obsidian is a prized material for making tools, because it can be chipped into a sharp point.

OCELOT A natural wildcat of Central and South America with a dark-spotted, brown coat.

ONYX A semiprecious stone that is black and white and made up of layers.

PATOLLI An Aztec board game that is very similar to modern-day backgammon.

PECCARY A nocturnal, piglike wild animal of North and South America.

PONCHO A blanketlike cloak with a slit in the middle for the head.

PYRAMID A massive memorial with a square base and four triangular sides.

QUETZAL A large tropical bird of Central and South America with golden-green and scarlet feathers.

QUETZALCOATL A legendary plumed or feathered serpent, worshiped by the Maya as a god of nature.

QUINOA A tiny, round, ivory-colored whole grain used by the Incas, and still eaten today. It is a complete source of dietary protein.

QUIPU An Incan counting device consisting of a length of cord held horizontally, with various knotted strings hanging down. Information was recorded according to the number of knots tied in the strings.

RITUAL The name for any customary observance or practice common to a people.

SACRIFICE The act of killing an animal or person in order to please a deity.

SARCOPHAGUS A stone coffin, or a stone container housing a coffin and a mummy.

The long, flowing tail feathers were prized for use in religious ceremonies

Quetzal

SPINDLE A stick or pin used to twist the yarn in spinning wool.

TEMPLE A religious structure built for the worship of a deity.

TERRACING In agriculture, a series of levels on a hillside, one above the other, used to greatly reduce the water erosion of soil.

TERRA-COTTA An unglazed fired clay, used for architectural features, ornaments, vessels, and to create sculptures.

TURQUOISE An opaque, blue, semiprecious stone with a porous, soft texture, prized in Mesoamerica.

TZOMPANTLI A skull rack placed outside a temple; for example, to hold the skulls of sacrifical victims.

UICTLI An essential farmer's tool; a digging stick made from strong, long-lasting wood with a long, broad blade carved into one end.

Tzompantli at Chichen Itza

ULAMA The sacred ball game, played in Mesoamerica by the Aztecs, Maya, and earlier civilizations.

VICUÑA A small, wild, cud-chewing animal similar to a llama but smaller; valued for its fleecy coat.

VIGESIMAL Relating to, or based on, the number 20, as in Mayan mathematics.

WHORL A circular arrangement of three or more leaves or flowers, equally spaced around the stem like spokes on a wheel.

Index

Acknowledgments

The publisher would like to thank:
Dra. Mari Carmen Serra Puche and all those who helped with photography at Museo Nacional de Antropología, Mexico City; Professor Eduardo Matos Moctezuma and all those who helped with photography at the Great Temple Museum, Mexico City (INAH-CNCA.-Mex.); Phil Watson at the Birmingham Museum; Maureen Barry at the Royal Museum of Scotland; British Museum; Pitt Rivers Museum; Cambridge University Museum of Archaeology and Anthropology; Reynaldo Izquierdo (Mexico) and Eugene Staken for photographic assistance; Sue Giles at the City of Bristol Museum; Jabu Mahlangu, Manisha Patel, Jill Plank, and Sharon Spencer for design assistance; Katharine Thompson; Lic. Victor Hugo Vidal Alvarez and Lic. Javier Garcia Martinez at the Tourist Office, Mexico City; John Woodcock and Andrew Nash for illustrations.
Additional photography: Geoff Dann (24ar); Steve Gorton (39al); Peter Hayman (60cl; 60c); Dave King (61bc); James Stephenson (14bl; 62-63 top; 63bl); Jerry Young (61ar; 61cl).
Index Lynn Bresler
Proofreading Miranda Smith
Wall chart Peter Radcliffe, Steve Setford
Clip art CD Jo Little, Lisa Stock, Jessamy Wood
Picture credits

The publisher would like to thank the following for their kind permission to reproduce their photographs:

(Key: a-above; b-below/bottom; c-center; f-far; l-left; r-right; t-top)

Ancient Art and Architecture Collection: 51 acr; The **Art Archive:** 38 ar; **Biblioteca Medicea Laurenziana,** Florence: 14acl, 48al, 51c; **Biblioteca Nazionale Centrale,** Florence 21al/Photo Scala: 35cl, 37al; **Bibliothèque de l'Assemblée nationale, Paris:** 30bl, 56bl; **Bridgeman Art Library:** Biblioteca Nacional, Madrid: 62cl; British Library: 17c, 19al; British Museum: 54bl; e.t. archive 26c, (detail, Diego Rivera 'Tarascan Civilisation') 42c; Museum of Mankind (detail: Diego Rivera "La Civilisation Zapotheque") 9bl, (detail, Diego Rivera "Cultivation of Maize") 24bc, (detail: Diego Rivera "The market of Tenochtitlan") 53bl; Private Collection: 63br; **Bristol Museums and Art Gallery:** 29br, 46c, 49bl, 62br; © **The Trustees of the British Museum:** 33 acr, 47 ar; **J. L. Charmet:** 37bl, 44bl; **Bruce Coleman Ltd.:** 16ar, 19ar, 60ar, 61al, 61ac; **Corbis:** Archivo Iconografico, S.A. 67tr; Nathan Benn 66tr; Bettmann 67bl, 67br; Jonathan Blair 69br; Bohemian Nomad Picturemakers 64tl; Don Conrad 64bl; Sergio Dorantes

70-71; Macduff Everton 68–69; Randy Faris 66b; Kevin Fleming 69tl; Werner Forman 64–65, 70b; Angelo Hornak 65tr; Charles & Josette Lenars 67tl; Gianni Dagli Orti 64br, 65cl, 69cl; Jose Luis Pelaez, Inc. 68tl; Bill Ross 71br; Kevin Schafer 65bc; Roman Soumar 68bl; e.t. archive: 22c, 32al, 38c, 40cr, 51br, 57c, 58al; Archaeological Museum, Lima: 20bl, 38br, 51br, 58bl; Arteaga Collection, Lima: 15cr; Museo Ciudad Mexico/ Sapieha: 12ac; University Museum, Cuzco: 10ar; **Mary Evans Picture Library:** 33cl, 45ac, 62bl/Explorer: 40al; **Werner Forman Archive**/Anthropology Museum, Veracruz: 9ar; **Getty Images:** AFP: 69bl **Robert Harding Picture Library:** 11bl, 17ac, 18cr, 18bl; Michael Holford: 16c, 17ar, 33bl, 54br, 56al; Hutchison Library: 59ar; Dorig: 7ar, 30cl, 34a; Pate: 17ac; **Linda Whitwam** © CONACULTA-INAH-MEX. Authorized reproduction by the Instituto Nacional de Antropologia e Historia: 70tr **Edward H. Merrin Gallery, New York:** 45ar; **Museum Für Vülkerkunde, Vienna:** 49cr; **National Geographic Stock:** Marial Stenzel: 35 ar; **National Museum of Anthropology, Mexico City:** 33cl, 45ac, 62bl/Explorer; Lima, Peru: 59acr; **NHPA:** Bernard: 13acl; Woodfall: 19b; **Rietberg Museum, Zurich:** 10bl; **Nick Saunders**/ **Barbara Heller:** 18c, 19acl, 23al, 31ar, 63ar; **Photo Scala:** Museo d'America, Madrid: 6br; **South American Pictures:** 13al, 13br, 15bc, 18cl, 18ar, 27al, 27acl, 30ar, 33ar, 34c, 40bc, 42al, 43ac, 57ar; **Hubert Stadler:** 68cr; **Michel Zabé:** 9ar, 30–31, 36bl, 47acl, 49c, 50al, 51ar, 52bl, 52c/NMA, Mexico City: 29al.

Wall chart:
Dorling Kindersley: Dave Rudkin © Dorling Kindersley, Courtesy of the Birmingham Museum and

Art Galleries 1bc, 1crb (bag), 1fcra; © The British Museum 1br (coins); Michel Zabe © CONACULTA-INAH-MEX. Authorized reproduction by the Instituto Nacional de Antropología e Historia. 1bl, 1ca, 1clb, 1crb (book), 1tl; Andy Crawford © Dorling Kindersley, Courtesy of the Pitt Rivers Museum, University of Oxford 1cb; © Dorling Kindersley, Courtesy of the University Museum of Archaeology and Anthropology, Cambridge 1crb, 1crb (counting device); Demetrio Carrasco © Rough Guides/Dorling Kindersley 1cl; Michel Zabe 1cr; **Getty Images:** Bridgeman Art Library 1br; Robert Harding 1tr

Jacket:
Front: Alamy Images: britishcolumbiaphotos.com (ca). **DK Images:** Andy Crawford/Pitt Rivers Museum, University of Oxford (tcl); Michel Zabe/ Conaculta-INAH-MEX/Instituto Nacional de Antropología e Historia (ca, tl, and ALB tr). **Getty Images:** Stone (cb).
Back: DK Images: Andy Crawford/Royal Museum of Scotland, Edinburgh (ca); Dave Rudkin/Birmingham Museum and Art Galleries (crb); Michel Zabe/ Conaculta-INAH-MEX/Instituto Nacional de Antropología e Historia (car, cb, cbr, cra, l).

All other images © Dorling Kindersley.
For further information see:
www.dkimages.com